RESTORED OHIO

Restored Ohio

History Brought Back to Life

PHOTOGRAPHS BY GLENN MORRIS
AND WILLIAM A. CRAFT

America Through Time®
ADDING COLOR TO AMERICAN HISTORY

America Through Time is an imprint of Fonthill Media LLC
www.through-time.com
office@through-time.com

Published by Arcadia Publishing by arrangement with Fonthill Media LLC
For all general information, please contact Arcadia Publishing:
Telephone: 843-853-2070
Fax: 843-853-0044
E-mail: sales@arcadiapublishing.com
For customer service and orders:
Toll-Free 1-888-313-2665

www.arcadiapublishing.com

First published 2019

ISBN 978-1-63499-121-6

Typeset in Mrs Eaves XL Serif Narrow
Printed and bound in England

DEDICATION

This book is dedicated to Ohio's pioneers and town founders. Without their efforts, courage, and persistence, Ohio wouldn't be the amazing state it is today. There are so many great places to explore and things to do. Whenever you think you've finally seen it all, something else pops up around a corner you never looked in before.

Acknowledgments

Publishing books requires the time and hard work of so many individuals whose passion for literature drives the industry. First and foremost, I thank Jay Slater of Fonthill Media for granting me the opportunity to publish my research and exploration finds in book form. Without Jay's restless pursuit of quality content, none of this would have been possible. Thanks also go to Alan Sutton, Kena Longabaugh, Matthew Rodriguez, and everyone else at Fonthill Media. I greatly appreciate the energy and enthusiasm of everyone at Arcadia Publishing, which manages the marketing and sales. My family, friends, group members of the Ohio Ghost Town Exploration Co., and citizens of The Great Buckeye State who pass their love of Ohio's history onto the next generation also have my heartfelt thanks.

Introduction

Old buildings and structures face many perils and possible demises such as demolition, fires, and being reclaimed by nature without sufficient care. Unless a building or structure is out in the middle of nowhere, the tendency in this region of the world is normally to demolish them when they get old to make way for redevelopment. Due to that practice and to the relatively young age of the state and country in comparison to other places around the world, anything built over one hundred years ago is old, over two hundred years is very uncommon, and structures over three hundred years are almost considered to be ancient these days. Ohio has an awesome abundance of both abandoned and restored historic locations and structures to explore.

In my first book, *Abandoned Ohio* (2018), we dove into the abandoned buildings and towns around the state in the hopes that at least some of what is left of them will be preserved for future generations to learn about and enjoy. *Restored Ohio* is based on the same concept, and some of the stories in both books interconnect. Most of the buildings in this book were abandoned or closed at one time or another but have since been restored and given a new lease on life to house and entertain citizens and visitors. Their fragile existence can require a lot of maintenance, and restoration costs can be very expensive, but preserving historic buildings and towns increases travel, tourism, and pride for state history. The National Register of Historic Places began with the National Historic Preservation Act of 1966, documenting and awarding structures with recognition on their list.

A big percentage of the current and former towns in Ohio were founded by Revolutionary War and War of 1812 veterans. The research I conduct on restored locations is done in exactly the same manner as the abandoned ones. I always try to find who founded or platted a town and who owned the buildings, what life was like for them, when they were born and passed away, and where they were buried. To me, those bits of information are all part of the larger story and complete my understanding of their significance. As with my first book, the towns are classified into categories: ghost towns, semi-ghost towns, small towns, and historic towns.

With the main focus of this book being about restored locations, most of the towns are categorized as small or historic; however, it also contains a decent number of ghost towns in areas that have since been repopulated and renamed. The picture captions contain GPS coordinates that can be typed into satellite map search bars to see exactly where they are and how to get there. They aid in planning trips and knowing more of what to expect before heading out. While cruising around Ohio on road trips or walking around any location, I always recommend looking for certain types of signs.

One kind of sign to keep an eye out for is the Ohio shaped corporate limit markers, usually on the outskirts of towns and on roads leading into them. They always have interesting facts like when the town was founded, who the famous residents were, or what the town's most popular historic attraction is. Another neat type of sign is the many Ohio Historical Markers which the Ohio Historical Society dedicates to places that are important to the state's history. They're brown with bronze borders and have a bronze outline of Ohio on the top with buckeye nuts and leaves. County and town historical markers are usually smaller, don't have the Ohio outline on top, and can be found in a variety of colors.

After the main body of this book containing the picture content, I included a businesses and organizations directory with website listings for anyone who wants more information on them such as their address, phone number, and hours of operation. Aside from the general historic nature of this book, it's also intended to be used for ideas for day or weekend trips. Several of the locations, especially the historic towns, require more than a day to explore all of their cool sites. They're great for individual and family trips, and interesting destinations for lovebirds to get to know each other more or rekindle their longtime romance. Some of the locations are also available for weddings and family reunions.

Transportation has always played a major role in shaping Ohio's towns and history. Flatboat travel by river was the easiest way into the state during the early days. Areas that weren't accessible by water were usually settled later and required travel by horse or walking to get to them. Construction on the Ohio & Erie Canal began in the 1820s to deliver people and goods to through places that were previously unsettled. Many farming and logging boom towns popped up along the canal routes. Stagecoaches dominated transportation until railroads were abundant in the mid-late 1800s and automobile travel surpassed the railroads well before the mid-1900s. For anyone reading this book in the distant future, gasoline combustion engine travel is still the main form of transportation for Ohio's citizens and was used to complete my works.

Glenn Morris
Ohio Ghost Town Exploration Co.

Harshaville Covered Bridge, GPS Coordinates: 38.907902 -83.543911

Harshaville, Ohio (Adams County)—Classification: small town

Built in 1855, Harshaville Covered Bridge crosses Cherry Fork on a picturesque drive through the countryside on Graces Run Road. Paul Harsha (1800-1876) and Martha (Buchanan) Harsha (1810-1884) moved to Ohio from Pennsylvania in 1841. They were farmers, raised livestock, and purchased a grist mill on Cherry Fork in 1846, later adding a saw mill to it. The town was subsequently named after them and had a post office from 1865-1909. Harshaville and the surrounding communities mostly consist of Amish residents who sell some of their fine homemade goods locally. Paul and Martha were buried with relatives in Unity Cemetery on Wheat Ridge Road.

Wickerham Inn, GPS Coordinates: 38.970451 -83.394271

Palestine, Ohio (Adams County)—Classification: ghost town

Revolutionary War veteran Peter Wickerham (1756-1841) and Maria (Platter) Wickerham (1767-1839) moved from Pennsylvania to Ohio in the late 1790s. They purchased a farm at the intersection of State Route 41 and Adkins Road. Back then, that portion of State Route 41 was part of Zane's Trace, an early pioneer road that stretched from Wheeling, West Virginia to Maysville, Kentucky. Realizing the importance of the location they chose to settle, Peter and Maria constructed the first brick house in the county in 1800-1801 with the idea of turning it into a tavern and inn for weary travelers along the road.

Locust Grove Cemetery, GPS Coordinates: 38.978293 -83.385185

They platted the town in 1837. It had a school, blacksmith shop, and a church. The inn was the only continually successful business in Palestine. It remained in operation until about 1850 and was used to help escaped slaves hide out on the Underground Railroad. Morgan's Raiders, a Confederate Army cavalry unit, rode through Palestine on July 15, 1863 during the American Civil War. Some of its soldiers stayed at the Wickerham Inn before continuing on their journey. Peter and Maria had nine children and were buried with relatives in Locust Grove Cemetery at the intersection of State Route 41 and Cemetery Road north of the inn.

Peter & Maria Wickerham Gravestone, GPS Coordinates: 38.978252 -83.387379

The cemetery was established in 1800 and the town of Locust Grove was platted in 1835. Palestine couldn't keep up with the growth of Locust Grove in the late 1800s. The same was the case with Peebles, which was platted to the south of Palestine in 1881 and quickly boomed with a newly laid railroad rolling through that area. Palestine didn't have any accommodations at the time to attract travelers or more residents and faded out of existence in the mid-1900s. Shortly before the town disappeared from maps, a local legend resurfaced and still captures the attention of readers and listeners to this day.

An old tale of the inn being haunted suddenly regained relevance nearly a hundred years after its origin. As the story goes, a stagecoach driver who was thought to be carrying a large sum of cash was murdered in the upstairs room he rented for a night, but his body was never found. Reports by locals and travelers of seeing a headless man in the window of the room were usually dismissed as a ploy to draw more visitors to the inn and town. In 1922 while the inn was getting renovated, workers moved limestone slabs of the basement floor and discovered a headless skeleton underneath them. It's considered by many to be the most likely haunted building in the county.

Olde Wayside Inn, GPS Coordinates: 38.794944 -83.547349

West Union, Ohio (Adams County)—Classification: small town

The Olde Wayside Inn at 222 W Main Street was initially called the Bradford Tavern. It was built in 1804 by General David Bradford, the same year West Union was founded. He achieved the rank of general in the Ohio Militia and was a smart entrepreneur. On top of running the hotel and tavern, David also operated a stagecoach service along Zane's Trace from Maysville, Kentucky to Chillicothe, Ohio. It always stopped at the Wayside Inn and gave him a leg up on the local competition with places such as the Wickerham Inn and Revolutionary War veteran John Killin's tavern at Killinstown, just a few miles east of West Union on State Route 125.

The Bradford Tavern was sold a few times over the passing decades of the 1800s. It was called the Marlatt House in the 1840s-1850s. From 1860 to the mid-1880s the inn was owned by John Crawford and went by the name Crawford House. John paid J. A. Caldwell, a well-known map publisher, to put an engraving of the building in the 1880 Illustrated Historical Atlas of Adams County, Ohio. William and Grace Lafferty purchased the tavern in 1936 and renamed it the Olde Wayside Inn. The current proprietor, Teresa Witten, is maintaining the tradition of keeping the building in operation.

Ruggles, Ohio (Ashland County)—Classification: small town

One of the most beautiful and well-known restored houses in the state was built in 1878 by Charles Crittenden (1845-1932) and Eliza (Crumrine) Crittenden (1847-1929). It's on US Route 224 about a half mile west of US Route 250. The prosperous 665-acre farm owned by the Crittenden family was internationally known for its sheep raising capabilities. The house consists of fifteen rooms and was constructed at the cost of $3,125. It's listed on the National Register of Historic Places along with seventeen other buildings, structures, and an unimproved lot on the site.

Castle Hill Crittenden Farm, GPS Coordinates: 41.029157 -82.426781

Georgetown Historic District, GPS Coordinates: 38.865638 -83.904351

Georgetown, Ohio (Brown County)—Classification: historic town

Allen Woods (1767-1862) immigrated to the United States from Ireland and married Hannah (Galbreath) Woods (1767-1852) in Pennsylvania. They moved to Ohio in 1803-1804. Allen platted Georgetown along what is now State Route 125 with twenty-two lots and two outlots in 1819. It quickly acquired more plat additions from local landowners and became the county seat in 1821. The town was attracting everything it needed, including mills on White Oak Creek, grocery stores, hardware stores, blacksmiths, and doctors. Public buildings such as new schools and churches were constructed whenever necessary. The population was at 618 in the 1850 census.

It was stated in the 1883 History of Brown County, Ohio that Georgetown's growth was slow but steady. The town had a train station on the Cincinnati, Georgetown, & Portsmouth Railroad from 1886-1936, but its arrival and existence didn't create a major population boom for the town. Businesses usually did well in the town square and were rarely unoccupied. The Georgetown Historic District was added to the National Register of Historic Places in 1978. It consists of seventeen acres with forty-two buildings and offers an alternative to the normal shopping experiences of the era. Parking is free in the town square and many historic structures are within walking distance.

In accordance with agreeing to be the county seat, Georgetown's first courthouse was built in 1823 and eventually needed to be replaced. A much larger courthouse was completed in the town square in 1852. During the Civil War, and on the same day they reached the Wickerham Inn, a Confederate detachment of 200-300 of Morgan's Raiders cavalry unit took control of the town square while stealing horses and goods from stores and residents. Long after surviving that day, a section of the courthouse was destroyed in an arson fire in 1977. Local citizens formed the Brown County Courthouse Reconstruction Association and raised funds for restoration. The courthouse was rededicated in 1982.

Ulysses S. Grant Boyhood Home, GPS Coordinates, 38.865888 -83.901904

General of the Union Army in the Civil War and eighteenth president of the United States, Ulysses S. Grant, spent his childhood in Georgetown before leaving for the West Point Military Academy in 1839. His father Jesse Grant (1794-1873) and mother Hannah (Simpson) Grant (1798-1883) saved up $1,100 in Point Pleasant, Clermont County. They moved to Georgetown and built their family home on Grant Avenue in 1823 when Ulysses was just a year old. Jesse owned a tannery across from the house and ran a construction business. He was the mayor of Georgetown from 1837-1839.

U.S. Grant Schoolhouse, GPS Coordinates: 38.862092 -83.903037

The Grant's home was purchased by John and Judy Ruthven in 1977. They donated it to the state in 2002. The house was declared a National Historic Landmark by the federal government and a total restoration was finished in 2013. The school Ulysses attended is restored on S Water Street. Both are museums run by the Ulysses S. Grant Homestead Association. Georgetown is also home to the annual Brown County Fair. The population in 2010 was 4,331. It's one of few old towns in Ohio that can boast of never having a lower 10-year census count than the prior one.

Ripley, Ohio (Brown County)—Classification: historic town

Built in 1867 on US Route 52, The Centenary United Methodist Church in Ripley is one of the town's most impressive buildings. Ripley was founded by Revolutionary War veteran Colonel James Poage (1760-1820) and Mary (Woods) Poage (1766-1830). James received 1,000 acres in Ohio from the state of Virginia for his military service. The family moved to Ohio in 1804 and built a cabin next to the Ohio River near the bank of Red Oak Creek. A few years later, James platted the town of Staunton, named after Staunton, Virginia. It was renamed Ripley after General Eleazer Wheelock Ripley (1782-1839), a hero of the War of 1812.

Centenary United Methodist Church, GPS Coordinates: 38.747264 -83.846292

Civil War Cannon at Union Township Public Library, GPS Coordinates: 38.745497 -83.845463

Ripley became an important shipping point for crops getting transported to other towns along the Ohio and Mississippi Rivers. Corn raising, tobacco farming, and pork packing were the main sources of income for local residents. In 1860, the Ripley Gas Light & Coke Company installed gas-powered lights in seventy-five homes and sixteen streetlamps, making it one of the first night time illuminated towns in the state. When the Civil War began in 1862, Ripley's old fairgrounds were used to muster and train Union Soldiers. A rare restored cannon from the period sits on the lawn of the Union Township Public Library at the corner of US Route 52 and Main Street.

The 1870s were probably the peak of Ripley's heyday. It had multiple mills, a lumber yard, two boatyards, a hotel, pork packing and slaughterhouses, two cooper shops, several churches, and a large tobacco warehouse. There was also a train station on the Ohio River & Columbus Railroad in the first couple decades of the 1900s. Much like its nearby neighbors of Levanna and Higginsport, Ripley didn't get big businesses in the 1900s to create a population boom in that century. However, it did maintain much of its population which is around 1,750 today. The old business district still bustles with activity, including the restored Bristow Pharmacy across the intersection from the library.

Bristow Pharmacy, GPS Coordinates: 38.745639 -83.845182

There are several historical markers and restored buildings around town. Some of the restored houses perfectly retain their charming bygone era looks. A historical marker on N Front Street has info about river town life in the 1800s. There's also a marker at the Union Township Library that has a story about the Civil War and the restored cannon in the yard. James and Mary Poage were buried in Old Ripley Cemetery next to the bank of Red Oak Creek in the woods at the intersection of 4th and Cherry Streets, where the end of 5th Street once was.

W.L. Johnson Carriage Factory, GPS Coordinates: 38.866811 -83.786301

Russellville, Ohio (Brown County)—Classification: small town

An extremely uncommon sight in Ohio is the restored W. L. Johnson Carriage Factory built in 1850 on State Route 125 in Russellville. Although carriage factories were abundant in the horse and buggy days, just a few of the original ones survived into the new millennium. Civil War veteran William Johnson (1838-1921) and Cindora (Shaw) Johnson (1845-1917) owned the factory and had five children. Cindora was a granddaughter of Russell Shaw (1781-1864) and Josanna (Reynolds) Shaw (1779-1864) who founded the town in 1817. William and Cindora were buried with relatives in Linwood Cemetery on the east side of town on Russellville-Winchester Road.

Howe Tavern, GPS Coordinates: 39.567440 -84.814846

College Corner, Ohio (Butler & Preble County)—Classification: small town

Gideon Sears Howe (1799-1875) and Sarah (McClay) Howe (1808-1883) purchased a section of land on US Route 27 from Miami University in Oxford in 1832 and built a stagecoach stop with a tavern and inn. They platted College Corner in 1837 and sold the tavern in 1840. Successive owners continued similar operations into the 1970s. The building was added to the National Register of Historic Places in 1976. It's currently listed on airbnb.com for overnight stays. College Corner was never a large town, but the strategic location on the townships border with Indiana has always kept it intact. The current population is around 400 residents.

Hueston Woods Covered bridge on Camden College Corner Road was constructed in 2012. It's 108 feet long and spans Four Mile Creek. This late 1800s wooden replica replaced an aging iron bridge that was built in 1929. The wide road lanes and tall roof clearance accommodate most automobile traffic while pedestrian sidewalks on each side grant access to cross the creek or hang out for a moment to enjoy the view. There's also a nice picnic area on the east side of the bridge, and Hueston Woods State Park offers many activities such as camping, hiking, golfing, and mountain biking.

Hueston Woods Covered Bridge, GPS Coordinates: 39.592005 -84.770219

The Hitching Post Saloon, GPS Coordinates: 39.496299 -84.661903

Darrtown, Ohio (Butler County)—Classification: small town

The Hitching Post on State Route 177 is another former stagecoach stop that still engages in its traditional business of distributing liquid refreshments. Abraham Darr (1784-1852) was the first settler in the area and built a general store. His brother Conrad Darr (1767-1832) and Catherine (Trig) Darr (1775-1840) from Pennsylvania arrived in Butler County in 1802. They had twelve children over twenty-three years and founded Darrtown in 1814. Abraham opened the tavern and inn in 1817, a post office at his store in 1825, and constructed a distillery in 1832. The town also had a school, two churches, a saw mill, grist mill, wagon shop, and several other small businesses.

St. Matthew Lutheran Church was dedicated in 1845. It has undergone some restoration and is a beautiful building north of The Hitching Post on State Route 177. Darrtown suffered from a lack of speedy transportation to attract large businesses after the stagecoach era ended and never had a canal or railroad. The advent of the automobile and local road improvements in the 1900s made stopping in town unnecessary for travelers. Its current population is approximately 500 residents. Abraham, Conrad, and Catherine Darr were buried with family members in Darrtown Pioneer Cemetery, established in 1806 west of town on Shollenbarger Road.

St. Matthew Lutheran Church, GPS Coordinates: 39.498493 -84.661919

Bethel Historical Society & Museum, GPS Coordinates: 38.963552 -84.080823

Bethel, Ohio (Clermont County)—Classification: small town

Obediah Denham (1747-1817) and Mary (Ball) Denham (1753-1818) ventured from New Jersey to Ohio to start a new life on American frontier. Their settlement was originally called Denhamstown and was platted as Plainfield in 1798, named after Obediah's hometown. It was replatted as Bethel in 1802. The Grant Memorial Building on State Route 125 started out as a school in 1930 and currently houses the Bethel Historical Society and Museum. It features exhibits with local, state, and national history and honors veterans and famous citizens who lived in the town. The building was restored earlier this decade and reopened in 2014.

Americans have enjoyed a love affair with movies for over a hundred years now. The first movie theater in Ohio opened in Bethel in 1908 and was operated by Aaron Little. The Midway Theater hit the scene in the late 1930s and was a big hit in its day. The single-screen venue could seat an audience of up to 400 at a time. It's located in the business block across State Route 125 from the museum and closed and reopened a few times in recent years. Silver screen legend Robert Redford did some filming at the Midway Theater in April of 2017 for the 2018 film *The Old Man & The Gun*.

Bethel Feed & Supply Pet & Garden Center, GPS Coordinates: 38.963871 -84.085207

Wichard Oil is a family owned gas and service station that opened in 1932 and was also used as a filming location. The building next to it is the Bethel Feed & Supply Pet & Garden Center. The three-story mill was constructed in 1858 and is an iconic building in town, despite not getting any direct attention in the movie. It's one of the oldest feed mills still in operation in the state. They are a common sight in Ohio's small towns, with many of them surviving the test of time, but most are used for other purposes these days.

Obediah and Mary Denham donated land for the Early Settlers Burying Ground (Denham-Burke Cemetery) on the north side of town on State Route 133 and were buried there with relatives and county pioneers. It's nicely maintained and has several signs and markers dedicated to local citizens who helped shape Bethel's history. A large stone marker mentions the "Unknown Hunter" who is believed to be the first burial there. It also has a condensed version of the town's beginning. As with most cemeteries in Ohio that are over 200 years old, the Early Settlers Burying Ground has many military veteran burials from the Revolutionary War to modern conflicts.

Early Settlers Burying Ground, GPS Coordinates: 38.968281 -84.080579

Chilo River Museum at Lock #34 Park, GPS Coordinates: 38.789719 -84.131907

Chilo, Ohio (Clermont County)—Classification: small town

It was known as Mechanicsburg prior to 1816 when Robert Bagby Jr. (1770-1818) laid out Chilo with 349 lots including a park and market space. The town was an important shipping port for steamboats in the mid-1800s and had two coal yards, several general stores, tobacco warehouses, a blacksmith, shoemaker, livery, and a hotel. The Chilo Lock 34 Visitor Center and Museum at 521 County Park Road off of US Route 52 has three floors of exhibits on Ohio River history. Admission and parking are free.

The museum building was constructed as the lock and dam powerhouse in 1925. It was restored by the Clermont County Park District in 2005. There's a set of restored steam engines out in the front yard from a former coast guard boat that was later converted into the USS Nightmare, a local Halloween attraction. The boat sank in 2005 but the engines were saved to be put on display. Chilo was flooded and nearly totally destroyed in 1887, 1913, and 1937. The population peaked at 200 in 1880 and was at sixty-three in the 2010 census. Robert Bagby Jr. was buried in Chilo Cemetery on State Route 222 north of town.

Lucy Run School, GPS Coordinates: 39.043533 -84.192144

Lucy Run, Ohio (Clermont County)—Classification: small town

Lucy Run was first settled by Charles Robinson (1763-1846) and Asseneth (Martin) Robinson (1768- 1835). They made the journey to Ohio from New England in 1806. Charles was a farmer and built a church in 1808 that was later moved to Amelia and became its Methodist church. Lucy Run also had a one-room schoolhouse that sits next to the town's infamous cemetery. The school has been restored and is currently a private residence on Lucy Run Cemetery Road. A county historical marker near the roadside has a lot of neat information on the schools of that time period.

Lucy Robinson, who was either a daughter or niece of Charles and Asseneth, was engaged to be married in 1806 or 1807. Her fiancé showed up at the Robinson cabin one day and told Lucy the bad news: he couldn't marry her because he was in love with someone else. After he left, the distraught Lucy mounted a horse and rode after him in an unlikely attempt to change his mind. A bad storm was rolling through the area and Lucy fell off her horse and drowned in the swollen creek between her family's cabin and the land that would become Lucy Run Cemetery.

The unsubstantiated legend claims Lucy was buried in an unmarked grave in the Robinson family plot of the cemetery. The hamlet and creek were later named Lucy Run and the road still bears her name to this day. Lucy can supposedly be seen at night running in a white gown from the creek to the cemetery, or from the cemetery and across the creek to where the Robinson cabin was, looking for her estranged lover. It's one of the most popular ghost stories in Clermont County and might be one of the oldest in the state, passed down by word of mouth for nearly two centuries before making it into cyberspace for all to read.

Moscow Food Pantry, GPS Coordinates: 38.858076 -84.229016

Moscow, Ohio (Clermont County)—Classification: semi-ghost town

Another neat old town on US Route 52 along the Ohio River is Moscow. It was founded in 1816 by French immigrants and initially thrived in conducting business with the other towns on the river. A school for women was constructed in 1844 at the corner of Wells Street and Fourth Street. It originally had three floors and has since been reduced to two. The Freemasons used it as a meeting hall for a few decades. They moved into a different building and put this one up for sale in 2013. It's now the Moscow Mission Food Pantry and has had some restoration over the last few years.

Fee Villa, GPS Coordinates: 38.856272 -84.232630

As if the continual threat of flood wasn't enough, a tornado ripped through Moscow in May of 2012. It destroyed an estimated eighty percent of the town and killed three residents. A lucky building that was spared massive damage was the Fee Villa on Broadway Street next to the river. The beautifully restored house was owned by Thomas Fee Jr. (1801-1862) and was a stopping point for escaped slaves on the Underground Railroad. Thomas was indicted for slave stealing by a grand jury across the river in Pendleton County, Kentucky but the governor of Ohio refused to extradite him.

Moscow Restored Tank in Veterans Park, GPS Coordinates: 38.855922 -84.231498

Moscow's heyday was around 1890 with 591 residents. That number is down to about 190 today. As the citizens recover from another natural disaster, the town proceeds to appreciate its history. A small park at the intersection of Broadway Street and Second Street has a few war memorials. One of them is a flag stand with plaques naming residents who died bravely in battle during the Civil War, World War I, World War II, and the fourth side has Korea, Vietnam, and Desert Storm. A restored M60A3 battle tank from the late 1960s sits nearby and is an impressive piece of history, the likes of which aren't normally seen in towns of that size.

Nicholsville Grocery, GPS Coordinates: 38.958429 -84.169619

Nicholsville, Ohio (Clermont County)—Classification: small town

Some small towns still need their own grocery store. This one on State Route 222 near the intersection of Bethel-New Richmond Road has a long history. Daniel Fee opened up a general store and post office at the location in 1825. Elisha Smith Dole (1814-1845), whose family sold Daniel his property, had six acres around the store divided up and sold for town lots. He named it Feetown in 1842. Nathan B. Nichols bought the store in 1843 and became the postmaster. The town was renamed Nicholsville in 1847. Members of both the Fee and Nichols families also owned stores in several other Clermont County towns during their early days.

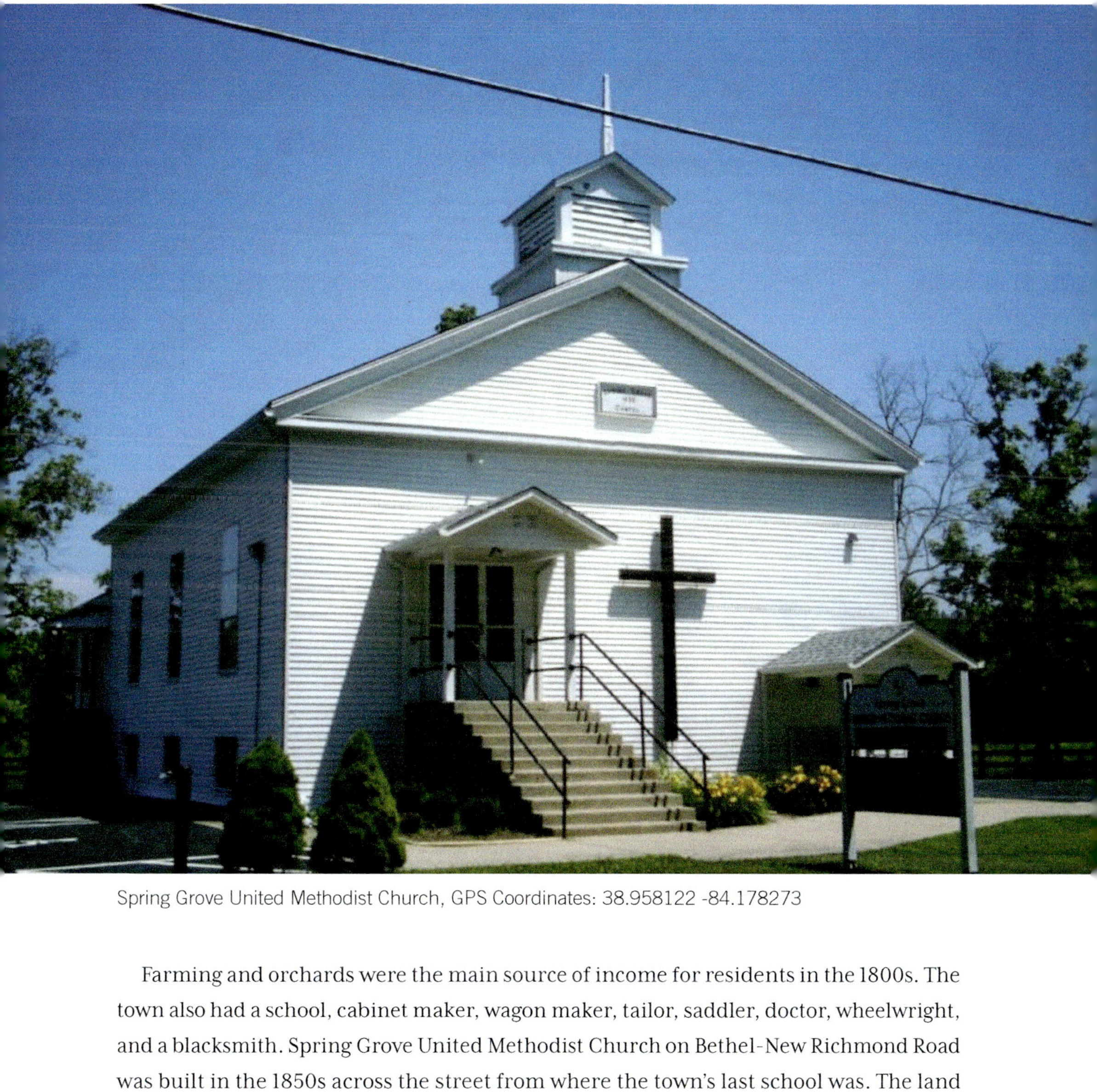

Spring Grove United Methodist Church, GPS Coordinates: 38.958122 -84.178273

Farming and orchards were the main source of income for residents in the 1800s. The town also had a school, cabinet maker, wagon maker, tailor, saddler, doctor, wheelwright, and a blacksmith. Spring Grove United Methodist Church on Bethel-New Richmond Road was built in the 1850s across the street from where the town's last school was. The land was once owned by the Roudebush family, who owned extensive orchards. Residents and pioneers were buried in Nicholsville Cemetery in the middle of town on State Route 222. The Hudson Fuel & Oil Co. across the street from the cemetery was founded by George and Barbara Hudson and has been in business since 1972.

Owensville Village Hall, GPS Coordinates: 39.122702 -84.136481

Owensville, Ohio (Clermont County)—Classification: small town

Owensville has been hosting the Clermont County Fair since 1864. It was originally called Boston and was platted in 1836 on a former land grant owned by Revolutionary War veteran and first US Surgeon General Dr. Richard Allison from New York (1757-1816) and Rebecca (Strong) West (1777-1828) from Connecticut. Richard was the first doctor in Cincinnati in 1789 and Rebecca was widely known as Cincinnati's most intellectual and beautiful woman. The town was renamed after William Owens who was the first postmaster. The village hall on US Route 50 is one of the most interesting buildings in Owensville. It started out as a Methodist Episcopal church in 1859.

The building currently houses the police department and village council. It's said to be haunted by the ghost of a woman named Nellie who straightens things up and cleans at night. On a personal side note, my grandparents Joseph Morris (1907-1993) and Leora (King) Morris (1910-1990) were the first paternal generation of my family to reside in Clermont County. They met at a one-room schoolhouse they attended in Kentucky, moved to Ohio around 1930 and had eight children. The last house they lived in was next to the Sunoco gas station on US Route 50 in Owensville. I spent many of my childhood days there and have good memories of the town.

Jonah's Run Baptist Church, GPS Coordinates: 39.496117 -83.980085

Jonah's Run, Ohio (Clinton County)—Classification: small town

Revolutionary War veteran Daniel Collett (1752-1835) and Mary (Haines) Collett (1753-1826) had nine children and were prominent landowners and farmers. They built a log cabin in 1814 and donated four acres along State Route 73 for public use. Daniel and Mary's children helped establish Jonah's Run Baptist Church congregation in 1838. The church was built in 1839 and has been added onto and restored a few times. Its accompanying cemetery is about the same age, with stones arranged in very straight rows close to the church. The Collett family wasn't part of the Quaker Society of Friends, like many of the other residents in the area, but they had similar beliefs about alcohol temperance and six of the Collett's sons married Quaker women.

Jonah's Run Baptist Church and three local farmhouses were listed on the National Register of Historic Places in 2006 as the Underwood Farms Rural Historic District. The Underwood Family ran the most successful farms in the hamlet. One of their houses, The West Brick, across from the Ohio Renaissance Festival complex on Brimstone Road, was constructed in the early 1850s. On top of growing crops and dairy production, Zehpaniah and Matilda Underwood owned an extensive 70-acre apple orchard. A barn from the enterprise still exists behind their East Brick residence on State Route 73 next to the church.

Underwood Farms Historic District, GPS Coordinates: 39.500163 -83.983100

Historic Roscoe Village, GPS Coordinates: 40.279199 -81.876410

Roscoe, Ohio (Coshocton County)—Classification: historic town

The nearly abandoned town of Roscoe Village received a second chance when it was restored and annexed into the City of Coshocton, which was once its rival directly across the Muskingum River. Roscoe was originally called Caldersburg, settled by James Calder in 1816. James was a merchant whose business failed in Coshocton. After building his cabin on the other side of the river, James had a 24- by 50-foot log tavern and hotel constructed on the land and platted Caldersburg with sixty-seven lots. Another brick tavern was built in 1821 and more businesses followed later that decade. Caldersburg had a post office from 1825-1831.

The town's boom hit when the Ohio & Erie canal arrived. Construction began in 1827 and was completed in 1830. A church and a new post office were built in 1831. That same year, the town changed its name to Roscoe, after William Roscoe (1753-1831), a popular English author. The Walhonding Canal was built from 1836-1842. It stretched northwest to the edge of Coshocton County and connected to the Ohio & Erie Canal at Roscoe. When it was completed, Roscoe became one of the most important shipping centers on the entire canal system in Ohio. Many of the townspeople would come out to greet new boat arrivals.

Roscoe Village Sweets & Treats, GPS Coordinates: 40.279800 -81.876231

In the 1840s Roscoe had five dry goods stores, two saw mills and flour mills, two grocery stores, a grain warehouse, and every other kind of business that towns needed in that era. Unfortunately, the town lost its railroad hopes as the city of Coshocton was chosen for a station on the Wheeling & Lake Erie Railroad and the Pittsburgh, Cincinnati, Chicago, & St. Louis Railroad (Big Four). Roscoe's worst fear came in 1913 when its canal system was almost totally destroyed in the massive flood that year. The town continued to lose population over the next few decades and the post office was disbanded in 1961.

A few years later, Edward and Francis Montgomery started efforts to restore the aging businesses and homes in Roscoe. The Roscoe Village Foundation was formed, which did an awesome job restoring the historic district! Although Roscoe is in the city of Coshocton these days, it still has its own identity and small-town charm. As with the other historic business districts in this book, parking is free and most of the fun is within walking distance. Many of the restored buildings from the town's early times have signs with building dates and historical information, making exploring and learning about the area very easy.

Caldersburg Pearl Canal Boat, GPS Coordinates: 40.277447 -81.877024

Canal boat rides on the *Monticello III*, which is pulled by draft horses, are offered from May-September at the landing at 23253 State Route 83. Starting from the north and heading south on N Whitewoman Street, Triple Locks Park is the first cool place to check out. It has more information about the canal system and is a great spot for a picnic. The Roscoe Village Visitors center is near the intersection of N Whitewoman Street and State Route 83. They have souvenirs and can tell you absolutely anything you'd need to know about the town and local annual events.

A restored canal boat, the *Caldersburg Pearl* built in the 1840s, is on the west side of N Whitewoman Street on the southern end of the historic district. There are also many other restored items and devices from the 1800s nearby, and around town, that add to the ambiance and bring history back to life. Roscoe is the perfect destination for a day or weekend trip, and the feel of the location changes over the course of the year. After going once, you might want to return in a different season to check out what else goes on there.

Unusual Junction, GPS Coordinates: 40.284669 -81.705246 (Photo Courtesy of William A. Craft)

West Lafayette, Ohio (Coshocton County)—Classification: small town

A unique roadside stop on US 36 east of Roscoe Village is definitely an unusual place, to say the least! In the early 1970s, Jerry and Jean McKenna purchased 120 acres of farmland that was formerly near a lock along the Ohio & Erie Canal and turned it into a tourist attraction. Jerry restored a barn on the property and called it the Unusual Shoppe, selling antiques and locally made food and goods. In 1976 he purchased a train station that was built in 1895 in Fredericktown in Knox County on the B & O Railroad, fifty miles northwest of its present location.

The McKennas bought the station in a disassembled pile and had to use old pictures of it to ensure the accuracy of the reconstruction. Old railroad cars on a track were attached to the building and surely increases travelers stopping by out of sheer curiosity. The business name changed to Unusual Junction in 1978 when Jerry converted it into a specialty shop, restaurant, and deli. It's open daily from 10 a.m.-6 p.m. and the Lava Rock Grill restaurant serves guests from 11 a.m.-2 p.m. Monday through Friday and 11 a.m.-4 p.m. on Saturday and Sunday. The Universal Bridal and Prom Superstore next to Unusual Junction has designer gowns and dresses for any special occasion.

Before going into the Unusual Junction store, there are lots of unusual things that catch the eye. One of them is Lady Liberty, proudly perched facing the highway. You can also get a closer look at the train and some other restored items from the long-gone railroad era. An extremely small chapel next to the bridal shop is likely only used for photographic purposes. The inside of Unusual Junction isn't just a store and restaurant. It's filled with all sorts of restored antiques, pictures, murals, and a few interesting oddities. The space almost overwhelms the senses with pure Americana.

(Photo Courtesy of William A. Craft)

A sign from the country's longest running television game show, *The Price Is Right,* was autographed by former host Bob Barker and put up for bidding at charity auction in 2009. It's 14 by 18 feet, weights almost 900 pounds, and had to be shipped by truck in pieces from Los Angeles. Many visitors can't resist getting their picture taken with it. Just up the road from Unusual Junction, McKenna's Farm Market at the intersection of US 36 and County Road 93 opened in July of 2018. It has fresh produce, a deli, salads, and some items made by the family, including salad dressing and pickles.

Bear's Mill, GPS Coordinates: 40.106781 -84.541899

Bears Mill, Ohio (Darke County)—Classification: small town

Bears Mill was settled by Revolutionary War and War of 1812 veteran Major George Adams (1767- 1832) and Elizabeth Adams (1773-1847). They had a saw mill and corn cracker built on Arcanum Bears Mill Road in 1832, but George died later that year. A new mill was built on the same spot in 1848 by local contractor Manning Hart (1821-1891). He sold it in 1849 to Gabriel Baer (1791-1859) and Charlotte (Spangler) Bear (1801-1887), a successful milling family from Pennsylvania. Gabriel finished the new mill including the wood siding that still lines the outside today.

The mill is the oldest industrial business in Darke County and was used as a meeting place for several decades in the mid-late 1800s. Residents and visitors would gather for picnics, toss horseshoes, and chat about news. It's unknown when and exactly why the name of the mill and town were changed to Bear. The mill was likely going to be removed by an amusement park that wanted to purchase the land, but it was saved in 1978 by Terry and Julie Clark who restored and reopened it. The address is 6450 County Hwy 34 and phone number 937-548-5112. Business hours are Tuesday-Saturday from 11 a.m.-5 p.m. and Sunday 1 p.m.-5 p.m.

The store on the first floor sells flour for all kinds of baking and frying purposes, preserves, pottery, souvenirs, and other locally made products. The stones grind corn and wheat. Three sets of them were brought over from France by Gabriel Baer at a cost of $6,000 per set, approximately $150,000 in adjusted inflation. Exploring the mill on a self-guided tour is nothing short of fascinating! Every floor is packed with historical machinery, 1800s antiques, and pictures and memorabilia from around the area. It's currently managed and maintained by the Friends of Bear's Mill, a non-profit organization that does great work in preserving the history.

Exploring outside the mill is also very interesting. It's powered by Greenville Creek with a dam and 2 turbines under the building's floor. The creek is thirty miles long and averaged a mill every mile in its heyday. Terry is a Vietnam Veteran. He acquired the former dome that was removed from the Darke County courthouse. It was headed for the scrap heap and Terry turned it into a Vietnam memorial with help from some of his friends. It honors the twenty-one citizens of Darke County who lost their lives in the conflict. The mill was also used to supply the Union Army with flour during the Civil War.

Anthony Wayne Peace Council House, GPS Coordinates: 40.106790 -84.634603

Greenville, Ohio (Darke County)—Classification: historic town

Located in Prairie Ridge Meadow Park on Wilson Drive across from the Garst Museum, this recreated log council house was dedicated in 1997 and aids in telling the story of the Treaty of Greenville and settlement of the area. The treaty between thirteen Native American tribes and the US Government was signed in 1795, ending the Northwest Indian War, and opening Ohio to further pioneer expansion. In respect of tradition, you enter the council house through the east door with the rising sun and exit through the west door with the setting sun. More information on tours is available from the Darke County Park District.

Washington Court House, Ohio (Fayette County)—Classification: historic town

The town was founded in 1810 and became the county seat in 1812. As with the Anthony Wayne Peace Council House, the unusual plat layout of Washington Court House has to do with the sun. Most towns in Ohio are platted "square with the earth". Streets normally run north-south and east-west. In Washington Court House, they're northeast-southwest and northwest-southeast, so all four sides of the courthouse building in the center of town get sunlight every day of the year. If platted in the typical manner, the north side of the courthouse wouldn't get any sun in winter.

Fayette County Historical Society Museum, GPS Coordinates: 39.538961 -83.435095

Fayette County's Historical Society Museum at the intersection of US Route 62 and US Route 22 is a restored Italianate style house that was built in 1875 by Morris Sharp (1838-1909), who was a well-respected banker and businessman. The 14-room house was purchased by the historical society in 1958 and renovated into a museum over the next few years. It's the third-tallest building in town and is only surpassed in height by the courthouse and St. Colman's Catholic Church. Morris reportedly wanted it to be designed as the showplace of the town. He was buried with relatives in Washington Cemetery on US Route 22.

Old Washington Cemetery, GPS Coordinates: 39.534062 -83.440840

The original town cemetery, called Old Washington, was established in 1810. It's next to the railroad tracks between Paint Creek and the northern side of S Hinde Street. The cemetery was reduced in size to its current half acre when the railroad was built. It has 112 headstones and many of the burials are Revolutionary War and War of 1812 veterans. It seems to have a relatively odd placement for such an old cemetery in a busy area, but the location was once at the southern edge of town and goes to show the growth of Washington Court House over its existence.

Mark Road Bridge, GPS Coordinates: 39.486961 -83.472988

Staunton, Ohio (Fayette County)—Classification: small town

Immediately behind buildings, bridges are my second favorite type of historical landmarks. On top of their wide range of architecture, their useful necessity keeps many old bridges intact and attracts restoration efforts. Mark Road Bridge crossing Sugar Creek off of US Route 62 in Staunton is a perfect example. It was constructed in 1883 and restored in 2007. The Mark family was the largest in the area and the road and bridge were aptly named after them. Half of the family lived in Jasper Mills in Jasper Township and the other half in Staunton, the only town in Concord Township.

The town was named by settlers from Staunton, Virginia. Michael Mark opened a blacksmith shop in the area in 1835. It was followed by a general store owned by Thomas Craig in 1842 and a post office in 1844. The town was platted in 1848. Residents had big hopes of getting a railroad someday but that never happened. As a result, the town's peak population of around 100 citizens hasn't changed much over time. Mark Family Cemetery is on the east side of Staunton Jasper Road and more members were buried in Staunton Methodist Church Cemetery on US Route 62 in town.

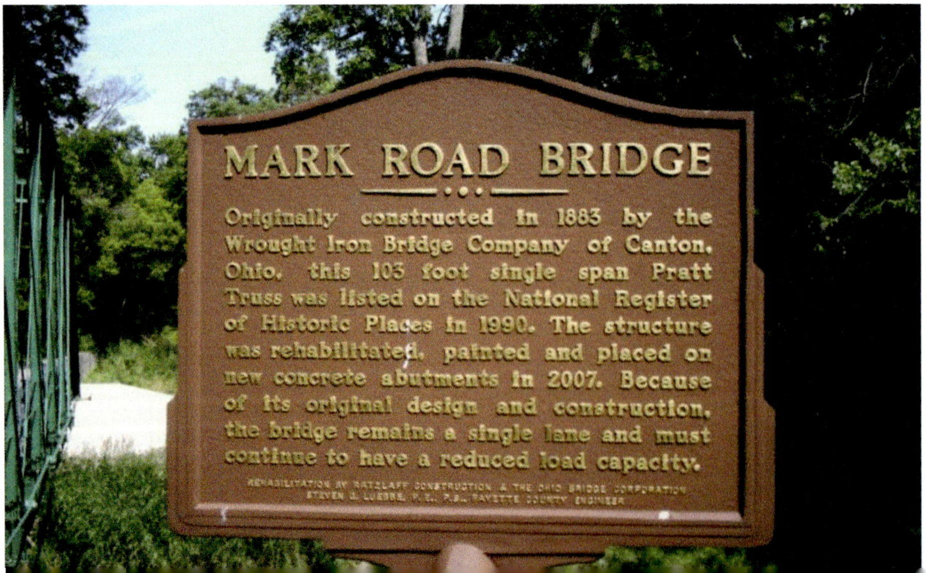

Fowler's Milling Company, GPS Coordinates: 41.529227 -81.256282 (Photo Courtesy of William A. Craft)

Fowlers Mills, Ohio (Geauga County)—Classification: historic town

Fowlers Mills was named after two brothers, Hiram Fowler (1800-1879) and Milo Fowler (1802-1860). They were born in nearby Burton, Ohio to parents from Connecticut and arrived in the area in 1829. Milo brought along his wife, Elanor (Foot) Fowler (1803-1875), and their two children. Hiram later married Minerva (Stone) Fowler (1809-1885) and had one child. The brothers built a millrace and saw mill along the Chagrin River on Fowlers Mills Road, followed by a grist mill that opened for business in 1835. As with Greenville Creek in Darke County, the Chagrin River is a powerful interior waterway that supplied plenty of power for numerous mills.

A couple years after building the grist mill, the Fowlers traded it for a wool mill. The town's post office was established in 1834 with Milo being the first postmaster. In 1837 Hiram was elected to one of the Munson Township trustee positions and Milo was a township treasurer. Milo constructed a new house for his family next to the grist mill in 1840. A marker for the Fowlers Mills Historic District is in the parking lot of the mill and has more information on the town and house. The two-story house was considered to be a frontier mansion when it was built, by far surpassing normal construction efforts of the time period.

The town also had a hotel, township hall, several stores, schools, and churches over the years. Hiram and Milo built more houses across the road from the mill in the 1840s. The one pictured above was constructed by Milo and the house below by Hiram. They're easily identified while cruising through town with wooden "Century Home" plaques next to the doors. More markers can be spotted around the area and are mostly metal plaques, indicating structures that are on the National Register of Historic Places. As with all of the historic towns in this book, it takes at least a good day to explore everything.

Fowler's Milling Company changed ownership a bunch of times. It was listed as the last operating flour mill in Munson Township in the 1878 History of Geauga And Lake Counties, Ohio. Charles S. Johnson purchased it in 1874. The mill was in bad shape by that time and needed a lot of repairs. Local residents were going to other mills in the county to get their grains turned into flour. Charles removed the turbine that powered the mill and replaced it with a 13-foot overshot water wheel with two sets of buckets for two sets of grinding stones. He also rebuilt the dam in 1877.

Fowlers Mills Christian Church, GPS Coordinates: 41.527419 -81.255549

Those improvements lasted until production stopped in 1966. Rick and Billie Erickson bought the property in 1985 and restored the mill, making it the last surviving grist mill in Geauga County. It's open Wednesday-Saturday from 10 a.m.-5 p.m. and closed on Sundays and holidays. The mill can produce 700 pounds of flour per hour from locally grown corn and wheat. The flour is sold in the mill store and nationally by mail-order. Visiting is an amazing experience and a great reminder that the state's best quality products aren't always obtainable from the giant chain grocery stores.

The town's cemetery is on the east side of Fowlers Mill Road north of the mill. It's a beautiful resting place and seems relatively small for the size and history of the community. Many residents were buried on family farm cemeteries. The gravestones of Hiram and Milo are in Bainbridge Township at Fowler Cemetery on the east side of Haskins Road between Taylor May Road and Crackel Road. It was officially established in 1825 but had some interments prior to that, like many other cemeteries in Ohio that were originally on farms. The earliest known burials there are from 1811.

Fowlers Mills Cemetery, GPS Coordinates: 41.532301 -81.256246

Alpha Mill & Museum, GPS Coordinates: 39.709647 -84.023699

Alpha, Ohio (Greene County)—Classification: historic town

The story of Alpha is also the story of the founding of Green County. It was first settled in 1803 by General Benjamin Whiteman (1769-1852) and Catherine (Davis) Whiteman (1775-1852), along with her parents Owen Davis (1751-1818) and Letitia (Phillips) Davis (1750-1824). They all later moved and founded Clifton. Benjamin built a log cabin tavern in Alpha and Owen built a grist mill. They began to hold meetings in the tavern with a few nearby residents and ended up turning it into the first courthouse in the county. The meetings included the founding and layout of Greene County, which they named after General Nathaniel Greene, a local Revolutionary War hero.

In 1827 another couple from Pennsylvania, John Harbine (1804-1873) and Hetty (Herr) Harbine (1806-1883), purchased the land that the mill and tavern were on. They employed many local residents and gave farmers better ways to process and sell their crops, mostly corn and tobacco. The Harbines and their children ran the grist mill, a saw mill, flour mill, wool mill, and a corn whiskey distillery. A post office was established in 1850. Tracks for the Panhandle line of the Pennsylvania Railroad and the Cincinnati, Hamilton, & Dayton Railroad arrived in the area in 1853. John and Hetty Harbine donated land for a train station.

Alpha was named after being the first village in Beavercreek Township. In 1854 along with their friend William J. Needles, the Harbines decided it was time to officially put the town on the maps and had it surveyed by Samuel T. Owens, the Greene County surveyor in Xenia. Frank C. Hubbell (1867-1949) and Hetty (Hagenbaugh) Hubbell (1870-1921) bought the Harbine's old farm in 1914 and added seven acres as a plat addition to the town. They founded the Alpha Seed & Grain Company. The building's office is now a museum. Alpha's current post office building was constructed in 1950.

A restored house built in 1900 sits across Alpha Road from the museum. It was used as a bed and breakfast as late as 2017, although I'm not sure if it's still in operation. If so, it would be a neat place to stay while in the area and a perfect starting point for exploring the town. Many of the state's former railroad track beds are now recreational trails with historic locations dotted along them. The 15-mile-long Creekside Trail bike route runs along the former railroad track line past the museum. It connects to the Little Miami Scenic Trail and Ohio-To-Erie Trail of the Miami Valley Trails System.

It's almost surprising that Alpha still retains its own name while being squeezed between Dayton, Beavercreek, and Xenia. The population is about 130 residents with fifty-four households who clearly love their town's history. Almost every house has had some restoration. History buffs must be careful while driving down Alpha Road, as they could easily twist a neck muscle with all of the head-turning sites. It's the smallest place in Ohio that we classified as a historic town. The properties are all very old but well taken care of, and some of the buildings have historical markers or signs with more information.

Aside from the locations already mentioned in this listing, there are a bunch more to check out. The town's last school on Alpha Road was built in 1883. Alpha Community Church in the center of town was constructed in 1872. John and Hetty Harbine's house at 751 Alpha Road has also been restored and has a historical marker. The log cabin tavern and courthouse built by Benjamin Whiteman was in the front yard. On an interesting side note, the Whiteman and Davis families reportedly moved out of Alpha disgruntled that the county seat was granted to Xenia. They founded Clifton in the hopes it would someday overtake Xenia, but that never happened.

Alpha School, GPS Coordinates: 39.712294 -84.019233

Old Stagecoach Inn, GPS Coordinates: 39.715706 -84.023525

Beavercreek, Ohio (Greene County)—Classification: historic town

The Old Stage Coach Inn on Dayton Xenia Road near the intersection of Beaver Valley Road was built about 1810 by Frank Stoll. It had a livery stable that could hold twelve to fourteen horses at a time and later turned into a blacksmith shop. One of the upstairs rooms was used as the town's high school from 1887-1888 while a new one was being constructed. The living room floor has a hidden door above a dirt dug out that is believed to have been used for hiding runaway slaves on the Underground Railroad. Several renovations were made to the building over the years, but it mostly still retains its original looks and charm.

Daytona Mills, GPS Coordinates: 39.723079 -84.056895

Shoup's Station, Ohio (Greene County)—Classification: ghost town

Solomon Shoup (1788-1812) was born into a family of millers from Maryland. He constructed Daytona Mills in 1805 along Little Beaver Creek two miles west of Alpha on a disbanded section of Old Mill Lane off of N Fairfield Road. It started out as a flour mill and is now a popular hardware store. The rebuilt mill was originally on the south side of the creek and was moved to the north side in 1921. Shoup's Station had a train station on the Dayton & Xenia Railroad with a general store and around fifteen residents. Solomon was buried with many relatives in Mt. Zion Shoup Cemetery at the intersection of N Fairfield Road and Indian Ripple Road.

Galloway Log House, GPS Coordinates: 39.687308 -83.930687

Xenia, Ohio (Greene County)—Classification: historic town

Revolutionary War and War of 1812 veteran Colonel John Paul (1758-1830) founded Xenia in 1803 and lobbied the commissioners to immediately locate the county seat there. A 257-acre lot was carved out for the town and surveyed by Joseph C. Vance, who bought the plat the next year for $250. Reverend James Towler proposed the name of Xenia, meaning "hospitality" in Greek. It required approval by vote from the town committee. The deciding vote was ironically cast by none other than Letitia Davis, whose family founded Alpha. A beautifully restored log cabin sits in the lot of the Greene County Historical Society & Museum at 74 W Church Street off of US Route 68.

The cabin was owned by Revolutionary War Veteran James Galloway (1750-1838) and Rebekah (Junkin) Galloway (1759-1812). They were married in Cumberland County, Pennsylvania and had ten children. The family moved to Fayette County, Kentucky where they met Daniel Boone, and James joined up in the resistance against the local Shawnee tribe. After participating in the siege of Old Chillicothe, at present day Oldtown in Greene County, James and Rebekah relocated their family there in 1798 and became friends with Tecumseh. Their daughter Rebakah (1791-1876) taught him how to read and write. The cabin was built in 1799 next to the Little Miami River, near what would later become Goes Station, and moved to its present location in 1965.

There are a bunch of other interesting old objects around the outside of the Greene County Historical Society Museum. One of my favorites was a small length of railroad tracks that shows the different gauges and types used in the area. Over on the N King Street side, a horse carriage step, water trough, and hitching post are neat examples of 1800s transportation related necessities. A call box behind the railroad crossing sign was used by the B & O Railroad to call the Pennsylvania Railroad to let them know they were there and ask if they could use the tracks. Several track mile markers are also in the lot.

The Galloway Log House was badly damaged in 1974 when a mile-wide category F-5 tornado destroyed much of the town and killed over thirty residents. Along with its restoration, the historical society saved a Victorian Era house that was relocated to the property in 1977. It was built by William and Florence McGervey in the mid-1870s and is called the Trebein-Flynn House, named after later owners. It's full of antiques and period furniture. The Greene County Historical Society Museum is open Tuesday-Friday from 12 p.m.-4 p.m. and Saturday from 12 p.m.-3:30 p.m. John Paul left Xenia and founded Madison in Jefferson County, Indiana where he lived out the rest of his life.

Five Mile Chapel, GPS Coordinates: 39.053422 -84.374569

Five Mile, Ohio (Hamilton County)—Classification: ghost town

Jacob Markely (1803-1879) and Emaline (Martin) Markley (1805-1870) donated land for Five Mile Chapel & Cemetery at 6977 Five Mile Road in Anderson Township. Jacob's parents, John Markley (1769-1841) and Mary (Springer) Markley (1756-1837), spent time in Maryland, Pennsylvania, and Virginia before moving to Ohio. John constructed a saw mill next to Five Mile Creek and used the lumber it produced to build cabinets and flatboats. The boats were used to ship goods from the area to towns on the Ohio and Mississippi rivers as far as New Orleans. Jacob and Emaline had 11 children and joined the family business.

The United Brethren congregation along Five Mile Creek built the church and officially established the cemetery in 1844. They used stones from the creek for the church construction with a limestone foundation and slate slab roof. It can be spotted on the 1847, 1869, and 1884 county maps. Five Mile Chapel has undergone some remodeling. Its front doors originally faced John and Mary Markley's graves. That changed when the bell tower was added in 1896 and the entrance moved to its base. Regular services ended in 1963 and it was added to the National Register of Historic Places in 1978.

The church and cemetery fell into disrepair for a while. Floods from the creek also damaged the building some over the years. It was adopted by the Five Mile Chapel Society who raised funds for repairs, maintenance, and upkeep. A creek wall was also constructed to prevent future flood damage. The cemetery is enclosed with a nice split log fence and has a historical marker for the Markley family. Events held at the church include an annual ice cream social and a Christmas gathering with carols and decoration making. The church also hosts around a dozen weddings every year and can seat sixty guests.

Miller–Leuser Log House, GPS Coordinates: 39.101557 -84.369940

Clough, Ohio (Hamilton County)—Classification: ghost town

An old hamlet along Clough Pike was settled in the late 1790s and named after Revolutionary War veteran and surveyor Richard Clough Anderson (1750-1826). It doesn't pop up on maps anymore and is considered to be in Newtown, although it's probably closer to Mt. Washington. The Miller-Leuser Log House was constructed on land formerly owned by Revolutionary War Captain Matthew Jouitt, who was granted 600 acres of land for his service. One of his sons contacted Nathaniel Massie to sell the property after Matthew passed away in 1793. Ichabod Miller (1774-1839) and Sarah (Mercer) Miller (1767-1832) bought 400 acres of the land along Clough Creek in 1796.

Their cabin at the intersection of Bartles Road and Clough Pike was built sometime around that year. It was occupied for over 170 years and changed ownership several times. Joseph and Matilda Leuser bought the property in 1907. Their newlywed son Lawrence Leuser (1889-1964) and his bride Emma (Kuntz) Leuser (1889-1969) moved into the house in 1910 and spent over fifty golden years together there. The Anderson Township Historical Society purchased it in 1971 and conducted the restoration. The outside lot has a historical marker with more information, an old barn, restored wagon, a GEM water well pump, and the original water well has been reconstructed.

Tours of the cabin are available on the first and third Sundays in June-October from 1 p.m.-4 p.m. and can be requested to be open for private tours and school trips. It's furnished with antiques and has been on the National Register of Historic Places since 1974. As Anderson Township celebrates its 225th anniversary, the old buildings around Clough have enjoyed some extra attention recently, with more events like walking tours and additional indoor activities. The town's last school was built in 1874 at the intersection of Clough Pike and Goldengate Drive. It's currently Clough Crossings Restaurant and features some historical exhibits and memorabilia from the area.

Clough Crossings Restaurant, GPS Coordinates: 39.096592 -84.368242

Clark Stone House, GPS Coordinates: 39.101557 -84.369940

Over at the corner of Clough Pike and Hunley Road, The Clark Stone House was constructed a few years after the Miller-Leuser Log House by Revolutionary War veteran and successful entrepreneur James Clark (1765-1852) and Savannah Clark (1765-1837). They moved to Ohio from Virginia and had ten children. James was a justice of the peace and served in the state legislature. One of their sons, Orson, lived in the house until 1854 when he sold it Adam Leuser (1819-1905) and Juliana (Fink) Leuser (1825-1892), a couple of hopeful immigrants from Germany. Joseph Leuser, who bought the log cabin down the road, was one of their sons.

Clough Baptist Church Cemetery, GPS Coordinates: 39.092907 -84.365613

Genevieve (Leuser) Messmer (1894-1978) and Joseph Messmer (1891-1984) inherited the stone house in 1923. Joseph was a florist and built a greenhouse next it. Three of the Messmer daughters sold the house to Anderson Township in 1995. A historical marker was placed in the front yard in September of 2018. As with the log cabin, it also has an old barn on the property and several other old objects of local and historical interest. The Greenfield Plant Farm next to the stone house at 6840 Clough Pike continues with the land's agricultural tradition and promotes its heritage.

Many of the town's residents and pioneers were buried in Clough Baptist Church Cemetery on Bridges Road, right around the corner from Clough Pike. The gravestone of James and Savannah Clark is in the left side in the corner on top of the hill. More information on the town, church congregation, and former church building is displayed at the entrance. Ichabod and Sarah Miller were buried with relatives in Columbia Baptist Church Cemetery on Wilmer Avenue in Columbia-Tusculum. Most of the Leuser family was buried in Guardian Angels Cemetery on Salem Road in Mt. Washington.

Loveland Castle Museum, GPS Coordinates: 39.283928 -84.265813

Loveland, Ohio (Hamilton, Clermont, & Warren Counties)—Classification: historic town

Loveland Castle, also known as Chateau Laroche, was built by World War I veteran "Sir" Harry Delos Andrews (1890-1981). He started its construction in 1929 and worked on the castle until his death which was caused by injuries from a trash fire on the grounds. The castle is named after a military hospital which Harry was stationed at during the war. Some of the castle is made from stones from the Little Miami River and the rest of it was completed with cement bricks molded from milk cartons. Harry is just one of several people who are said to haunt the castle. It's now a museum and is available for weddings, ghost hunts, and tours.

Ghost Town Roadside attraction, GPS Coordinates: 40.957779 -83.672056

Findlay, Ohio (Hancock County)—Classification: historic town

A roadside attraction on a quiet and peaceful stretch of County Road 40 off of US Route 68 south of town is deeply ingrained in the history of the area. Louis J. Galitza (1910-2000), who designed Frontiertown at Cedar Point in Sandusky County, began construction of Ghost Town amusement park in 1958. The recreated late 1800s town opened to the public in 1959 and entertained visitors for several decades. Louis's son Edward Galitza also helped build and run the establishment. Before completing the story of the amusement park, we'll go back and explore a bit of the land's history.

Elijah Woodruff (1806-1865) moved to Ohio with his parents and siblings in 1829. They were pioneers in the township and settled along Eagle Creek in Eagle Township. Elijah owned the 240-acre farm that eventually became the site of the Ghost Town roadside attraction. Elijah married Sarah (Walters) Woodruff (1819-1886). They had eight children and used sixty acres of the farm for growing crops. Elijah and Sarah built a large farmhouse, after living in a log cabin for a few years, and another house on the land for their son Sheldon Woodruff (1842-1923), who inherited eighty acres of the farm. He married Missouri (Alspach) Woodruff (1846-1935), had a few children, and continued farming the land.

Sheldon lived his whole life on the Woodruff farm and the family attended Pleasant Grove United Brethren Church at the intersection of County Road 40 and County Road 75. The area mostly comprised of farms and a few mills along Eagle Creek. It never had a busy 1800s village, until Ghost Town arrived. Louis Galitza moved half of the amusement attraction buildings to the property and the other half were constructed there as recreations. The oldest structure is a blacksmith shop from the 1820s. It also has every other normally imaginable type of building from the era, plus a cemetery and a dance stage.

Hired actors did gunfights and added to the atmosphere. There was also a steam train from 1919, a donkey corral, and two museums with over forty antique horse drawn vehicles. Annual crafts shows with vendors and operating it as a Halloween attraction helped put the amusement park on road maps an in travel guides. Ghost town reportedly got 30,000-50,000 visitors a year for several years before closing its gates after Louis Galitza passed away in 2000. The property was sold to a local man who had great memories of visiting when he was younger. It was restored with the help of the Boy Scout Troop from Camp Berry on the other side of Eagle Creek.

The pictures of Ghost Town in this book were taken prior to the restoration completion, but everything has been fixed up and repainted. Ghost Town is now back up and running! It still does the craft shows, Halloween attraction, has some new events, and is open for general business. It may be an attraction of a dying breed but has been given a second chance to entertain and is well worth a visit. The address in 10630 County Road 40 and phone number 419-270-2667. Elijah and Sarah Woodruff were buried with relatives and township pioneers in Bishop Cemetery on the west side of Trail 74 between County Road 37 and County Road 26.

Dodson Township Hall, GPS Coordinates: 39.202293 -83.816054

Dodsonville, Ohio (Highland County)—Classification: small town

Small towns dotted along Ohio's US and state routes usually have something worth stopping by to check out while cruising around on planned or random road trip. I usually look for keystones and plaques above doors or close to the roofs of buildings, which usually indicate they're of some sort of historic importance. Dodsonville was founded in 1839 and had a post office from 1843-1906. The Dodson Township hall on US Route 50 was built in 1917. It receives good maintenance and is one of a few public buildings left from the old town's heyday. Early residents were buried in Dodsonville (Lutheran) Cemetery at the intersection of State Route 134 and North Street.

Smith Tannery, GPS Coordinates: 39.352574 -83.379116

Greenfield, Ohio (Highland County)—Classification: historic town

General Duncan McArthur (1772-1839) founded Greenfield along Paint Creek in 1799. He was a War of 1812 veteran and the eleventh governor of Ohio. The Smith Tannery and residence at the intersection of State Route 28 and N McArthur Way is the oldest existing tannery in the state. It was constructed in 1821 by Revolutionary War veteran William Smith (1760-1836) and Catherine (Robinson) Smith (1751-1840). One of their sons, Samuel Smith (1793-1875), also helped with the construction and worked in the family business. His first wife, Nancy (Mitchell) Smith (1796-1816), passed away just a month after their first child was born.

Samuel M. Smith (1816-1874) was born in the tannery house and served as the Surgeon General of Ohio during the Civil War. The Smith family were abolitionists and used their house to help runaway slaves on the Underground Railroad. It was listed on the National Register of Historic Places in 1978. Across State Route 28 on S McArthur Way, the Travellers Rest Inn was built in 1812 and was the town's first stone building and post office. It's now a museum and sits next to the Old Burying Ground where William and Catherine Smith were buried with relatives. The Greenfield Historical Society is across from the tannery on N McArthur Way and features two train stations.

Greenfield Train Stations, GPS Coordinates: 39.353474 -83.379388

The Dayton, Toledo, & Ironton station was built in 1878 and operated until 1973. It has been restored and now houses the Greenfield Veterinary Clinic. The B&O station next to it was built in 1854 and closed in 1985. It was turned it into a museum by the historical society and has a cool model train and town display and other exhibits. Both of the stations were very important to Greenfield's economy in the 1800s and throughout the 1900s, providing quick transportation for goods and citizens. The population is presently over 4,500 residents and continually presses the threshold of being a city. There're also many other historic sites around town to explore.

Hillsboro, Ohio (Highland County)—Classification: historic town

Opera houses were a big part of entertainment around the state in the 1800s and early 1900s. In 1895 Bell's Opera House opened in Hillsboro on S High Street off of US Route 50. It held plays and musical performances in the days before motion pictures and was used by the high school for events and graduation. It was a movie theater for a decade or so before closing in the 1930s when it couldn't compete with newer theaters around the area or keep up with more modern fire code standards on visitor capacity. The building was restored in 2011 and has a row of businesses on the first floor.

Bell's Opera House, GPS Coordinates: 39.201685 -83.611696

Buckeye Furnace, GPS Coordinates: 39.056538 -82.457344

Buckeye Furnace, OH (Jackson County)—Classification: ghost town

Counties in southeast Ohio did just as well as other corners of the state with mills and farming. The region was also blessed with an abundance of coal and iron that began fueling the economy in the mid-1800s. Its effects spread from the local level, to the state, and country, producing iron and steel for modern construction, and jobs in several new industries that instantly created boom towns. Buckeye Furnace on Buckeye Park Road was built in 1851 and started blasting iron ore in 1852. The land was donated to the state in the 1930s and the Ohio Historical Society restored the entire site in 1972.

Typical furnaces in Ohio only required around a couple dozen workers to operate a furnace site. The size and scale of Buckeye Furnace is a lot to take in, and it's tough to imagine something that big being run by so few workers. The furnaces usually employed several hundred workers in related industries though, such as coal, iron, clay, and limestone mining. Transportation jobs also greatly increased as workers were needed to ship raw materials to the furnaces for production and ship the finished products away for sale. Railroads, boat businesses, horse wagon, and ox wagon businesses all benefited well from furnaces.

About seventy iron furnaces were scattered around the Hanging Rock Region of Ohio. Most of the ones that remain are in rough shape and were dismantled for scrap a long time ago. Some are toppled over and turning into piles of stones and faded memories. Examples of them can be found in my first book, *Abandoned Ohio* (2018). The only section that's usually left is the pyramid-shaped base. A vent shaft on the base of Buckeye Furnace gives a neat look at how the stones were cut and placed. Several of the original furnace buildings were restored including the charging shed, iron master's house, and a storage shed.

A replica of the Buckeye Furnace Office & Store is past the furnace on Buckeye Park Road. Most workers in the local industry were paid in company store tokens. The furnace was in operation twenty-four hours a day, 365 days a year. Whenever it wasn't blasting, it was getting prepared for another long run. It was a tough life at times but was steady work and pretty much guaranteed food and shelter. Buckeye Furnace also had a church, school, and a row of wood houses for the residents. The community was abandoned shortly after the furnace closed in 1894.

Office & Store, GPS Coordinates: 39.054699 -82.458141

Buckeye Furnace State Park is on 270 acres with picnic areas walking trails. The town's cemetery is up the hill behind the company store where some of the residents were buried. There are just a few tombstones left, but the cemetery has a lot more burials in unmarked graves. The furnace was added to the National Register of Historic Places in 1970. A covered bridge in the lot of the company store was built in 1872 crossing Raccoon Creek and made it onto the register in 1975. The museum and gift shop in the company store is open on Saturdays and Sundays in May-October from Noon-4pm.

Granville Historic District, GPS Coordinates: 40.067903 -82.519108

Granville, Ohio (Licking County)—Classification: historic town

In 1804 residents from Granby and Granville, Massachusetts formed The Licking Company and purchased over 29,000 acres of land in Ohio. Many of them were Revolutionary War veterans. A group of settlers arrived in 1802 and another 150 or so in 1805. They immediately began planning their new town with a 288-lot plat and decided on locations for all of the community buildings they would need. Granville enjoyed good growth and prosperity through the 1800s and early 1900s. Approximately 5,770 residents currently call the place home. Its historic district square is at the intersection of Main Street (State Route 661) and Broadway Street.

The Buxton Inn, GPS Coordinates: 40.067636 -82.516234

Orrin Granger (1788-1822) built a tavern and inn east of the town square on Broadway Street, which served as a stagecoach stop between Columbus and Newark. It was purchased in 1865 by Civil War veteran Major Horton Buxton (1821-1902) and Marion (Partridge) Buxton (1828-1901). Major Buxton owned the inn until his death and it still carries his name to this day. Everyone from presidents and celebrities, to us common folk, have visited the inn and drank in its downstairs tavern for over two centuries. The Buxton Inn is the longest continually operated hotel in Ohio. It also has amazingly low rates for the experience of a stay.

One of the other famous owners was Ethel "Bonnie" Bounell (1888-1960). She was a dancer, singer, and entertainer who operated the inn from 1934-1960. Her cat named Major, after Major Buxton, was the cat on the inn's longtime former roadside sign. The cat is reportedly said to appear around the inn by the workers and visitors. Ethel Bounell and Major Buxton are also reported to continue to hang out there. Ethel is referred to as "The Lady in Blue" for often wandering around in a blue dress. She is most likely to be seen in or near her room no. 9 upstairs but gets spotted in other places too.

Orville and Audrey Orr purchased The Buxton Inn in 1972 after they heard it might be demolished. They restored the buildings over the last few decades and we had the privilege of speaking with Orville for a while, who we unexpectedly met in the restaurant room on the main floor. He was quietly sitting by himself reading a newspaper, and after greeting us in a friendly manner, proceeded to tell us several of his own stories about the inn. It was an awesome experience and we give unending credit to Orville and Audrey for their love of The Buxton Inn and its history. It has since been sold and is under new management.

Ashley Azariah Bancroft House, GPS Coordinates: 40.066629 -82.518129

On top of the expected sites, many of the 1800s buildings on the side streets and secondary roads in Granville survived the test of time and are now on the National Register of Historic Places. They usually have small metal plaques next to their doors with more information. One of the nicest looking restored homes was built in 1825 and owned by Azariah Bancroft (1798-1885) from Granville, Massachusetts and Lucy (Howe) Bancroft (1799-1882) from Vermont. The Bancrofts moved to Missouri in 1841 and later out to Napa County, California where their lifelong journey west, always in true pioneer spirit, came to its end about as far west as it could possibly go.

Granville Train Station, GPS Coordinates: 40.064508 -82.520689

Granville had a few population booms with its large grain mill and the railroad industry. The train station from the Toledo & Ohio Central Railroad was built in 1880 and has been restored. It sits at 425 S Main Street. The former railroad track line is a bike path from Newark to Johnstown. Granville's mill is still in operation and runs a general store across from the train station. Education had always been important to the community. Log cabins weren't enough to accommodate the residents, so the town had a three-story brick school constructed before 1820. Granville had five schools before the 1830s rolled around.

Swasey Observatory, GPS Coordinates: 40.071139 -82.520867

A number of higher education schools and institutes were built in Granville over the years. Denison University's roots go back to 1831 and now has around 2,100 students. Swaysey Observatory at 300 Chapel Drive was built in 1909. It houses an astronomy library and is one of the coolest buildings on the campus, giving students and visitors closer views of the moon and space. The outside was constructed with beautiful marble. In 1970, its original dome was replaced, and the inside was remodeled. There are several historical markers around the area too, mostly dedicated to Granville's previous and continued commitment to education.

Old Colony Burying Ground, GPS Coordinates: 40.065608 -82.520340

The Granville Inn, across the road from The Buxton Inn, was completed in 1924 and is also reportedly haunted. A historical marker at the intersection of Broadway Street and Main Street tells the story of The Licking Company and early settlers. Another neat historical maker is on S Main Street next to the Old Colony Burying Ground where many of Granville's early settlers were laid to rest. The Buxtons were buried with relatives in Maple Grove Cemetery on E Maple Street. The town is a great trip for anyone who would like to spend a few hours or even a day or few visiting many different historic locations.

Ludwig Mill, GPS Coordinates: 41.415482 -83.862064

Providence, Ohio (Lucas County)—Classification: ghost town

Peter Manor (1778-1847) settled in the area in 1816. He was a fur trader who previously operated a trading post for the Northwestern Fur Company. Peter built a saw mill in 1822 next to the Maumee River and expanded it with a grist mill in 1835. He platted the town of Providence in 1837 and had to sell off his mill to the state in 1838 during construction of the Miami & Erie Canal. Most of the eighty-eight plats in the town, which were on five streets, were bought up and the area started to grow. Providence Dam was constructed in 1840 and was used to keep the canal full and level.

Canal Boat Ticket Booth, GPS Coordinates: 41.415359 -83.857505

Canal towns normally boomed with the shipping business, but a series of setbacks kept Providence from having great heydays like most other towns of its kind. Unfortunately, a devastating fire swept through the business district in 1846, causing an early population decrease. Peter Manor died the next year while in the process of rebuilding his mill. Isaac Ludwig (1813-1906) and his wife Christenia (Ness) Ludwig (1819-1903) purchased the mill and completed its construction. Providence was hit by the cholera epidemic in the early 1850s and the population decreased again. Many residents perished from the disease and some who survived left to avoid potentially getting it.

Providence lost its post office which ran from 1836-1868. It was also passed up by local railroads due to its successive early struggles. Parts of the canal system were reconstructed in 1906-1909, but the improvements of that effort were lost in the Great Flood Of 1913. By that time, the canal system was getting left in the dust by the railroads and automobile transportation anyway. Its eventual closing was pretty much the last straw for Providence. Local officials couldn't come up with any other ways to keep it going. Lucas County officially removed Providence from their recording list in 1928, instantly turning it into a ghost town at the time.

With the success of Grand Rapids on the other side of the Maumee River in Wood County, the Providence area was never totally abandoned. In 1930 The Toledo Metropolitan Board acquired the land that later became Providence Metropark. Its historic nostalgia made the Ludwig Mill and former canal a tourist attraction. The mill was added to the National Register of Historic Places in 1974 along with the historic district in 1975. Providence is still a populated place in Lucas County for census purposes but is listed on Google Maps as a ghost town, and the area has been annexed into Grand Rapids.

The Ludwig's Mill is restored and has a general store in Providence Metropark at 13827 US Route 24. It's open from May-October on Wednesday-Sunday 10 a.m.-5 p.m. On Sundays they have full demonstrations of the mill operations from 1 p.m.-4 p.m. A replica canal flat boat called the *Volunteer* passes through the abandoned Miami & Erie canal Lock No. 44. It's the only original canal lock in Ohio that's still functioning and serving its original purpose. The US Route 24 entrance to the canal boat launch is on the eastern side of the metropark. Its 8.3-mile-long Towpath Trail runs along the Buckeye Trail System.

There are also a few other old buildings in the Providence Historic District. Providence Dam Shelterhouse at the western side of the metropark was built in 1941. It's a two-story picnic venue with bathroom facilities overlooking the dam. The shelterhouse can be rented for weddings and family reunions and seats eighty guests. Some other remnants left from Providence can be found on the back roads north of US Route 24, including former one-room schoolhouses and family farm cemeteries. Isaac and Christenia Ludwig were buried in Mount Pleasant Cemetery on Bailey Road off of Providence Neapolis-Swanton Road about three miles north of town.

Germantown, Ohio (Montgomery County)—Classification: historic town

Settlers with German ancestry from Berks County, Pennsylvania began making their way to the vicinity in the first few years of the 1800s. Philip Gunckel (1766-1848) and Catharine (Shaeffer) Gunckel (1766-1836) led a group of twenty-four families by flatboat to Cincinnati, and then up to Hole's Station, later named Miamisburg. Philip was the only one who could speak English at the time. The Gunckels made a land speculation investment by buying up a bunch of the original lot recordings in the valley between Little Twin Creek and Big Twin Creek, founding Germantown in 1804. They had eight children and Philip was a miller.

Shuey Mill, GPS Coordinates: 39.621100 -84.370217

In 1806 the Gunckels built a saw mill and grist mill on their land. They platted Germantown in 1814 with the main street leading from the mill into the village. The mill was sold to the Gunckel's son-in-law Lewis Shuey in 1930. He rebuilt and enlarged the mill to three-and-a-half stories in 1845. A cigar manufacturing plant bought the mill in 1888 and also used it for a tobacco warehouse. Around that time, a two-story addition was attached to the right side of the building. It's presently operated as the Shuey Mill Inn & Event Center at 313 S Main Street and is available for weddings and large events.

The Florentine Hotel at 21 W Market Street (State Route 725) started out as a brick structure that was completed in 1816. It's currently the back portion of the former stagecoach stop and tavern. A couple of wood frame sections were added before 1860. Food was cooked for guests in the basement fireplace and traveled by dumbwaiter up to the restaurant on the first floor. The hotel had a few different names and forty-three owners over the course of its life. It closed in 1974 while needing a lot of repairs. It was purchased for renovation in 1976 and reopened as a restaurant in 1979.

The Florentine Restaurant, GPS Coordinates: 39.624902 -84.371088

Engine House Tattoo, GPS Coordinates: 39.626020 -84.369954

As with all of the historic towns in this book, I list many of the main attractions but also leave some surprises to be found by anyone who goes to explore them. After going to an intended destination, cruising around aimlessly and hitting the side streets in Ohio's old towns usually leads to neat places you didn't expect to run into. For me on this trip, it was Engine House Tattoo on E Center Street. The former firehouse was built in 1858 after the original one was destroyed in a fire. It was restored in 1996 and has been the tattoo shop since 2012.

State Road United Methodist Church, GPS Coordinates: 39.630293 -84.459770

In 1976 the area around the Florentine Hotel was added to the National Register of Historic Places as Gunckel's Town Plan Historic District. Germantown had a train station on the Cincinnati, Jackson, & Mackinaw Railroad. The station was built in 1896 and has been restored. It sits with a small length of tracks next to W Warren Street in Veterans Memorial Park. Philip and Catharine Gunckel were buried with relatives in Germantown Cemetery on State Route 725 west of town. Heading further into the outskirts of town, State Road United Methodist Church was built in 1920. The church and cemetery behind it are on land that was donated by relatives of Catharine Gunckel.

Old Dutch (Moyer) Cemetery, GPS Coordinates: 39.634682 -84.476167

Old Dutch (Moyer) Cemetery is a mile west of the church on the south side of State Route 725. It dates back to 1820s and is named after the Moyer family who owned much of the land in the area. Some of their ancestors arrived in Germantown with the Gunckels. Moyer Road, around the corner from the cemetery, is also named after them. The cemetery has about 100 interments. It was once overgrown but is now preserved with a chain link fence and a historical marker. The burial ground looked nicely mowed and all of the stones appeared to be in their rightful places.

Peninsula, Ohio (Summit County)—Classification: small town

The Connecticut Land Company had extensive interests in northern Ohio and sent surveyors to the area in the early 1800s. Peninsula was settled in 1818 along the Cuyahoga River and became an important boat stop on the Ohio & Erie Canal. Hermon Bronson (1774-1853) and Mary (Hickox) Bronson (1777-1858) moved from Waterbury, Connecticut to Ohio and located in the area in 1824. They had four children and platted Peninsula in 1837. Hermon built a saw mill and grist mill along the Cuyahoga River, a couple of churches, and a few other buildings around town. Bronson Memorial Church at 1712 Main Street was constructed in 1839.

Boston Township Hall, GPS Coordinates: 41.241613 -81.554575

Peninsula Train Station, GPS Coordinates: 41.242361 -81.548948

The Bronson House across the street from the church was built with locally-quarried sandstone.

Peninsula started out in Portage County and became part of Summit County when it was formed in 1840. The Boston Township Hall was built as a school in 1887 at a cost of $4,000. It combined two aging and inadequate one-room schoolhouses. The structure was expanded with a brick addition in 1920. Boston Township bought the building in 1939. A grange hall occupied the first floor for almost fifty years in the 1900s. After falling into disrepair, restoration began in 1990 and continued until recently with the roof getting an update.

Peninsula's heyday was in the 1880s when it peaked out at 5 hotels and 14 saloons. The town traded train stations with Boston Mills and is on the Cuyahoga Valley Scenic Railroad, which gets all decked out for Christmas and the holiday season with the Polar Express that runs in November and December. Train rides are also conducted throughout the rest of the year and run along track lines that date back to 1880. Ohio & Erie Canal Locks 28-31 in Peninsula were listed on the National Register of Historic Places in 1979. It's a beautiful small town with a ton of history and a population of 560 residents.

Zoar Hotel, GPS Coordinates: 40.612313 -81.422354

Zoar, Ohio (Tuscarawas County)—Classification: historic town

One of the coolest completely restored villages in the Ohio is on State Route 212 in Tuscarawas County. Its most recognized building is the reportedly haunted Zoar Hotel, built in 1833 on Main Street. Zoar was founded by immigrants who left Germany due to religious persecution from the Lutheran Church. They purchased 5,500 acres of land in Lawrence Township, in hopes of attaining a better quality of life. Joseph Bimeler (1778-1853) and Dorthea (Huber) Bimeler (1786-1852) founded Zoar along with 300 other settlers in 1817. It was named after the biblical city and means "sanctuary from evil." Joseph was a pipemaker, teacher, and the leader of the group which was called The Society of Separatists of Zoar.

The Bimeler Cabin is the oldest structure in town. It was built in 1817 on 4th Street and was used as the first meeting house. Much of the land was acquired by loans that needed to be paid back quickly. The society bought the land sight unseen, and upon arrival, immediately began working on trying to figure out exactly what to do with it. They needed to know what crops could grow well there and which ones were most worth their time with planting and harvesting. Paying off the land loans as soon as possible reduced their accruing interest and lifted fears of repossession.

Bimeler Cabin, GPS Coordinates: 40.614439 -81.423009

That goal became a source of motivation for the residents. On top of the financial stress, tensions ran high between the society members over several other aspects of life too. Most of those tensions were ironed out in their articles of association written in 1819. The society was much like an Amish community, although there were some differences. Women worked right alongside the men in farming and did equal work. According to the articles, no one had individual rights of property. Everything was done for the good of the community and the citizens were given "the necessities of life—nothing beyond."

A grist mill was built on the Tuscarawas River in 1821 to increase the town's revenue and a post office opened in 1826. The state bought up some of the Society of Separatists land for the right of way of the Ohio & Erie Canal in the 1820s. Jobs for constructing seven miles and four locks on the canal gave Zoar's residents the opportunity to quickly pay off the land loans, which they accomplished by 1830 along with construction of a wool factory. The society was incorporated by the state as an organization in 1832. Over fifty of the town's citizens died of cholera that year, but the population remained steady.

Tin Shop, GPS Coordinates: 40.614124 -81.422308

Zoar Elderly Home/Bimeler House, GPS Coordinates: 40.613259 -81.422349

New member applications reached the post office on a near daily basis. Joining the society was tough and required making it through a probationary period. Applicants had to conform to the lifestyle, but work was easy to get. The town bought an iron furnace in 1834 that employed around 100 families. The Number One House is another impressive building in town. It was intended to be a home for the elderly. The idea was later scratched, and it was given to the Bimeler Family. A second mill was built on the river in 1837. The community spread out into neighboring townships over the next few decades.

The Society of Separatists owned the train station on the Cleveland & Pittsburgh Railroad in nearby Fairfield, platted in 1854 on current-day State Route 800. It was called Zoar Station and had a general store and post office. Charles H. Ehlers (1839-1909) was the first postmaster. A group of members of the society platted Valley City with twenty-eight lots in 1882, just a quarter mile north of Fairfield. Thirteen more lots were added crossing the border into Sandy Township in 1883. The name of the train station and post office in Fairfield changed to Zoarville in 1914, combining the two towns into one.

The Bimeler Museum, GPS Coordinates: 40.613638, -81.423585

Back in Zoar, Joseph Bimeler's death in 1853 caused dwindling interest in the community life and the villagers voted to disband the Society of Separatists in 1898. The town's land was divided up between the remaining residents. A former house at the corner of E 3rd Street and Park Street was built as a house in 1863 and owned by William Bimeler (1876-1928) and Lillian (Ruof) Bimeler (1876-1942). Lillian donated the building to the Ohio Historical Society. They converted it into The Bimeler Museum in the early1920s. Zoar's historic district, which encompasses pretty much the whole town, was listed on the National Register of Historic Places in 1969.

Zoar Cemetery, GPS Coordinates: 40.617314 -81.427417

Other restored locations from the old village include the bakery, tin shop, wagon shop, blacksmith shop, dairy, and the kitchen and laundry. The garden in the middle of town is ornately planted. Historically, it has mostly been used for flowers and likely dates back to at least the 1820s. Zoar's first school on E 3rd Street is a bed and breakfast. The Zoar Village State Memorial site is managed by the Ohio Historical Society and The Zoar Community Association. The store and visitors' center is at 198 Main Street. Joseph and Dorthea Bimeler were buried in Zoar Cemetery at the end of 7th Street with most of the original society members.

Bigelow House, GPS Coordinates: 40.114961 -83.424398

Chuckery, Ohio (Union County)—Classification: small town

Chuckery was settled in the 1820s along Little Darby Creek. The unincorporated community, whose center is at the intersection of State Route 161 and State Route 38, never had a canal, railroad, or a major population boom. Farming has historically been the main source of income for residents. One of the largest families in Chuckery's early days was the Bigelows. They were relatives and descendants of Isaac Bigelow (1759-1822) who founded the nearby town of Plain City on Big Darby Creek. One of his nephews, Elphiaz Bigelow (1802-1864), constructed the Bigelow House which stands on State Route 161 close to the intersection of Ax Handle Rd.

The house was completed in 1846 and was the showcase of the town for many decades. Aside from that, Chuckery had a general store, a Methodist Episcopal Church also known as Lewis Chapel, a brick one-room schoolhouse, and later a high school. St. Paul's Lutheran Church Congregation formed in 1893 and ran a parochial school. Both the church and school were held in the same building during the congregation's early days. They built a wood frame church in 1902. The last class graduated from the town's public high school in 1937 and the Chuckery's last store went out of business in 1946.

Bigelow Covered Bridge, GPS Coordinates: 40.115668 -83.425246

A semi-truck crashed into the abandoned store in 1953. It was used for a fire practice exercise in 1961. St. Paul's Church was replaced with the present brick structure on State Route 38 in 1964. Bigelow Covered Bridge was built in 1873 crossing Darby Creek on Ax Handle Road to provide a direct link north to Marysville. It was named after Eliphas Bigelow. The bridge was restored in the 1990s and repainted in 2008. A historical marker on its southern end tells more of the story. Chuckery also had a post office from 1898-1903, which probably marked the end of its heyday. Since then the mail goes through Plain City.

The reverse side of the historical marker has information about the Darby Plains, considered to be one of Ohio's best stretches of farmland. Eliphas Bigelow was buried in Bigelow Pioneer Cemetery with many of his relatives and other early families from the area on Rosedale Road, south off of State Route 161. The surrounding land is called Bigelow Cemetery State Nature Preserve. It features native grasses and plants that covered Ohio's landscape prior to our modern yards which are full of Asian and African grasses. Most citizens spend a lot of time and money caring for them, but they aren't great ecosystems for wildlife or nature in general.

Corwin Town Hall, GPS Coordinates: 39.524811 -84.077538

Corwin, Ohio (Warren County)—Classification: small town

A tiny town hall at the intersection of Corwin Avenue and Purkey Lane was built in 1844 and used as the village's first council house and jail. The town was also platted around that time by John Johnson (1795-1846) from Virginia, and his son Joel W. Johnson (1819-1849). It was named after Thomas Corwin, the fifteenth governor of Ohio. Corwin had two train stations on the Little Miami Railroad, one for passengers and another for freight. The town hall was listed on the National Register of Historic Places in 2001. John and Joel were originally buried with relatives in Friends Burial Ground in Waynesville. Their graves were moved to Miami Cemetery on Corwin Avenue.

Old Log Post Office, GPS Coordinates: 39.559640 -84.306407

Franklin, Ohio (Warren County)—Classification: historic town

Founded in 1796 by pioneer and politician General William Schneck (1773-1821) from New Jersey, Franklin has grown well since its beginning and presently has about 11,800 residents. William married Elizabeth (Rogers) Schneck (1776-1853) in 1798 and had ten children. The family moved to Franklin in 1803. William was a militia general in the War of 1812 and a board member of the Miami Exporting Company, Ohio's first chartered bank. He also founded Newark and Toledo. Throughout his political career, William helped propel the Ohio & Erie canal from an idea into reality. He was appointed to a commission of three surveyors who charted the future canal's path.

Unfortunately, William contracted malaria during the canal surveying trips, turning one of his crowning achievements into his eventual demise. His family continued to have success and influence in Franklin though, including his brother John. Postal records are an integral part of researching current and former towns. The Old Log Post Office on S River Street in Franklin is the oldest existing one in Ohio. John Schneck (1778-1867) and Sarah (Tapscott) Schneck (1787-1842) had twelve children and opened a general store at their two-story cabin in 1802. It became the town's post office in 1805 and was added to the National Register of Historic Places in 1976.

Franklin's location along the Great Miami River and Ohio & Erie Canal made it a perfect place for many kinds of business opportunities and industries. Both farming and manufacturing drove the economy and attracted a couple of railroads. The town's Cleveland, Cincinnati, Chicago, & St. Louis (Big Four) train station was built in 1872. It has undergone some restoration over the years and is at the corner of S Main Street and E 6th Street. There are numerous other historical sites around town and the occasional mural with picturesque scenes of the area's earlier days. Woodhill (Franklin) Cemetery was established in the 1850s on Hamilton-Middletown Road.

Franklin Train Station, GPS Coordinates: 39.557529 -84.305677

The Golden Lamb, GPS Coordinates: 39.433765 -84.208422

Lebanon, Ohio (Warren County)—Classification: historic town

Another reportedly haunted former stagecoach stop in Lebanon rivals the Olde Wayside Inn, Buxton Inn, and Florentine Hotel in operating longevity. The Golden Lamb Inn at 27 S Broadway Street initially opened its doors to travelers in 1803, the year after Lebanon was founded. It was built by Jonas Seaman and Martha (Forbes) Seaman and named after a recognizable gold colored lamb on the building's sign, back in the days before reading and writing were expected abilities of the average citizen and passenger wagon operators. The structure started out as a two-story cabin and expanded to four floors around 1815.

Its location being halfway between Cincinnati and the National Road (US Route 40) made it a necessary stop for many travelers. Twelve US presidents have visited the inn along with other notable 1800s celebrities including Charles Dickens and Mark Twain. The inn conducts the same sort of business as it did over 200 years ago with a restaurant, tavern, rooms for overnight guests, and is also a museum with gift shop. It was listed on the National Register of Historic Places in 1978. Several ghosts are said to roam the halls and hang out in the hotel rooms. Tours and ghost hunts are offered to visitors at various times throughout the year.

Pioneer Village, GPS Coordinates: 39.485863 -84.037636

Henpeck, Ohio (Warren County)—Classification: ghost town

Quaker immigrants Levi Lukens (1767-1860) and Elizabeth Lukens (1763-1831) moved from Pennsylvania to Ohio in 1807 and settled in their cabin just south of Caesar Creek on January 1, 1808 and had seven children. The family's cabin and barn are restored and in what is now called Caesar's Creek Pioneer Village. Henpeck was a small town with about thirteen buildings and a saw mill and fulling mill on Caesar Creek. It was last seen in the 1891 Warren County Atlas but hasn't been found on any later maps. The community of Wellman started up just a mile south around the same time Henpeck was abandoned.

Its residents likely moved to get away from areas that flooded frequently, long before construction of Caesar Creek Lake in the early 1970s. The restored frontier town on Pioneer Village Road was established in 1973. It has a couple dozen historic buildings from the Caesars Creek area including a general store, blacksmith shop, school, sugar shack, and the Collett's Cabin from Jonah's Run in Clinton County. The village is accessible year-round for exploring outside, and the buildings get opened for festivals and events. Levi and Elizabeth Lukens were buried with relatives in Massie Township (Henpeck/Wellman) Pioneer Cemetery on the north side of Oregonia Road.

Waynesville Historic District, GPS Coordinates: 39.529700 -84.086766

Waynesville, Ohio (Warren County)—Classification: historic town

As a tribute to my favorite Ohio historian, Henry Howe (1816-1893), I will conclude the main body of this work by starting off with a paragraph written more in his style and personal tone. I arrived in Waynesville on the northeast side of State Route 73 on Thursday September 20, 2018. Although there were ample places to park that day, the streets were lined with the vehicles of business owners and shoppers. I imagined visiting on the weekend must be quite a scene, and much tougher to find empty parking spots. It was nice to see such an old town with so much modern interest its historic Main Street.

Waynesville was founded by Quaker settlers in 1796 and named after Revolutionary War veteran General "Mad" Anthony Wayne (1745-1796). Their journey by flatboat from Philadelphia over to Columbia in Hamilton County, Ohio and then up to Waynesville was documented by their guide Francis Bailey (1774-1844), an English scientist, astronomer, and adventurer. His book *Journal of a Tour in the Unsettled Parts of North America* was posthumously published in 1856. The Hammel House Inn at 121 S Main Street began with a log cabin called the Hammel House Stand around 1800. It was rebuilt with a wood frame structure in 1817. The bricks section was added in 1822.

Fire House & Lockup, GPS Coordinates: 39.532208 -84.085679

The building was renovated into apartments in the mid-1900s and turned into a bed and breakfast with a restaurant and gift shop in the 1980s. It's reportedly haunted by several ghosts, including a black shadowy figure said to have passed through the wall from room no. 2 into room no. 3 where a guest was staying. The Waynesville Engine House and Lockup at 260 Chapman Street was built in 1881 as the town's first fire station. An addition in the back was constructed in 1886 and used for the jail. It was added to the National Register of Historic Places in 1999 and was up for sale when I visited.

Museum at the Friends Home, GPS Coordinates: 39.531083 -84.089788

Over on S 4th Street at the intersection of Miami Street, the Museum at The Friends Home is another very impressive structure. It was built in 1905 by the Quaker's Society of Friends and was a boarding house for retirees and single teachers. The building is considered to be the gateway to the Quaker Historic District in Waynesville. The museum is open 1 p.m.-5 p.m. on Wednesdays and Saturdays from April-December. Tours for the Quaker Meeting House, constructed in 1811 next to the museum, are also available. In closing, citizens and visitors of the Great Buckeye State of Ohio have plenty of history to explore, both abandoned and restored!

Businesses and Organizations Website Directory

Adams County

Olde Wayside Inn—adamscountytravel.org/foodunique.html

Brown County

Grant Home & School—usgrantboyhoodhome.org/

Butler County

The Hitching Post—facebook.com/thp1817/

St. Matthew Lutheran Church—stmatthewdarrtown.com/

Clermont County

Bethel Historical Socitey & Museum—bethelmuseum.com/

Bethel Feed & Supply Pet & Garden Center—bethelfeedmill.com/

Wichard Oil—wichardoil.com/

Chilo Lock 34 Park—ohio.org/destination/historic-sites/chilo-lock-34-park

Moscow Mission Food Pantry—moscow-mission.org/

Spring Grove United Methodist Church—umc.org/find-a-church/church/60862

Hudson Fuel & Oil Co.—hudsonfueloil.com/

Clinton County

Jonah's Run Baptist Church—robertmackayclan.com/meetings/ohjonahsrun/

Coshocton County

Roscoe Village—roscoevillage.com/

Unusual Juction—theunusualjunction.com/

Universe Bridal and Prom Superstore—universebridalandprom.com/

Darke County

Bear's Mill—bearsmill.org/

Darke County Park District—darkecountyparks.org/

Fayette County

Fayette County Historical Society & Museum—fayette-co-oh.com/residents/museum.php

Geauga County

Fowler's Milling Company—fowlermill.com/

Greene County

Alpha Mill Museum—beavercreekohio.gov/Facilities/Facility/Details/Alpha-Mill-6

Daytona Mills—fernco.com/locations/united-states/retail/daytona-mills-inc/45432

Greene County Historical Society & Museum—sites.google.com/site/greenehistoricalsociety/

Hamilton County

Five Mile Chapel—fivemilechapel.org/

Miller-Leuser Log House—andersontownshiphistoricalsociety.org/page3.html

Greenfield Plant Farm—greenfieldplantfarm.com/

Loveland Castle—lovelandcastle.com/

Hancock County

Ghost Town—facebook.com/Ghost-Town-Findlay-Ohio-1525098627787387/

Highland County

Greenfield Historical Society & Museum—greenfieldhistoricalsociety.org/

Bell's Opera House—facebook.com/Bells-Opera-House-Hillsboro-Ohio-126007634100490/

Jackson County

Buckeye Furnace—ohiohistory.org/visit/museum-and-site-locator/buckeye-furnace

Licking County

Buxton Inn—buxtoninn.com/

Granville Inn—granvilleinn.com/

Denison University & Swaysey Observatory—denison.edu/map/places/swasey-observatory

Lucas County

Ludwig Mill—metroparkstoledo.com/explore-your-parks/providence/

Montgomery County

Shuey Mill Inn & Event Center—shueymill.com/

Florentine Restaurant—florentine-restaurant.business.site/

Engine House Tattoo—enginehousetattoo.com/

State Road United Methodist Church—umc.org/find-a-church/church/59384

Summit County

Cuyahoga Valley Scenic Railroad—cvsr.com/

Tuscarawas County

Zoar Village—historiczoarvillage.com/

Warren County

Golden Lamb Inn & Restaurant—goldenlamb.com/

Caesars Creek Pioneer Village—caesarscreekpioneervillage.org/

The Hammel House Inn—thehammelhouseinn.com/

Museum at the Friends Home—friendshomemuseum.org/

BIBLIOGRAPHY

County history books and maps published in the 1850s-1920s were the main resources used to compile this work. The history books contain firsthand accounts of what life was like for residents when the towns were organized and during their heydays. Smaller tidbits of information, such as genealogy and railroad records, were collected from various database style websites.

Adams County

Arms, Walter F. *Caldwell's Illustrated Historical Atlas of Adams County, Ohio*. J. A. Caldwell, 1880, www.historicmapworks.com/Atlas/US/11049/Adams+County+1880/.

Evans, Nelson W., And Emmons B. Stivers. *A History of Adams County, Ohio*. E. B. Stivers, 1900, books.google.com/books/about/A_History_of_Adams_County_Ohio.html?id=8HwUAAAAYAAJ.

Ashland County

Baughman, A. J. *History of Ashland County, Ohio*. The S. J. Clarke Publishing Co., 1909, https://books.google.com/books?id=QxgWAAAAYAAJ&printsec=frontcover&source=gbs_ge_summary_r&cad=0#v=onepage&q&f=false

Neiderheiser, F. L. *Map of Ashland County Ohio*. Wertman And Neiderheiser, 1897, https://www.loc.gov/resource/g4083a.la000598/?r=0.272,0.74,1.455,0.915,0

Brown County

Lake, D. J. And Griffing, B. N. *Atlas of Brown Co., Ohio*. Lake, Griffing & Stevenson, 1876, www.historicmapworks.com/Atlas/US/7674/Brown+County+1876/.

Morrow, Josiah. *The History of Brown County, Ohio*. W. H. Beers & Co., 1883, books.google.com/books/about/The_History_of_Brown_County_Ohio.html?id=udUyAQAAMAAJ.

Butler County

Bartlow, Bert, Cone, Todhunter, & Others. *Centennial History of Butler County, Ohio*. B. F. Bowen & Co., 1905, https://books.google.com/books?id=H283AQAAMAAJ&printsec=frontcover&source=gbs_ge_summary_r&cad=0#v=onepage&q&f=false

Everets, L. H. *Combination Atlas Map of Butler County, Ohio*. L. H. Everets & Co., 1875, http://www.historicmapworks.com/Atlas/US/9365/Butler+County+1875/

Clermont County

Hill, John. *Map of Clermont County, Ohio*. Williams & Dorr, 1857, www.loc.gov/resource/g4083c.la000607/.

Lake, D. J. *Atlas of Clermont County, Ohio*. C. O. Titus, 1870, www.historicmapworks.com/Atlas/US/11064/Clermont+County+1870/.

Lake, D. J. *Atlas of Clermont County, Ohio*. Lake & Gordon, 1891, www.historicmapworks.com/Atlas/Maps/US/11065/Clermont+County+1891/.

Rockey, J. L. *History of Clermont County, Ohio*. Louis H. Everts, 1880, babel.hathitrust.org/cgi/pt?id=yale.39002054234126;view=1up;seq=5.

Williams, Byron. *History of Clermont And Brown Counties, Ohio*. 2 vols. Hobart Publishing Company, 1913, books.google.com/books/about/History_of_Clermont_and_Brown_Counties_O.html?id=bdYyAQAAMAAJ.

Clinton County

Brown, Albert J. *History of Clinton County, Ohio*. B. F. Bowen & Company, 1915, books.google.com/books/about/History_of_Clinton_County_Ohio.html?id=6dYyAQAAMAAJ

Durant, Pliny A. *History of Clinton County, Ohio*. W. H. Beers & Co., 1882, books.google.com/books/about/History_of_Clinton_County_Ohio.html?id=771Cp_3FMB0C

Lake, D. J. And Griffing, B. N. *An Illustrated Atlas of Clinton County, Ohio*. Lake, Griffing & Stevenson, 1876, www.historicmapworks.com/Atlas/US/7588/Clinton+County+1876/

Coshocton County

Hill Jr., N. N. *History of Coshocton County, Ohio*. A. A. Graham & Co., 1881, https://books.google.com/books?id=9gzVAAAAMAAJ&printsec=frontcover&source=gbs_ge_summary_r&cad=0#v=onepage&q&f=false

Darke County

Griffing, B. N. *Atlas of Darke County, Ohio*. Griffing, Gordon & Co., 1888, www.historicmapworks.com/Atlas/US/8294/Darke+County+1888/

Lake, D. J. and Griffing, B. N. *Atlas of Darke Co., Ohio*. Lake, Griffing & Stevenson, 1875, www.historicmapworks.com/Atlas/US/9826/Darke+County+1875/

The Lewis Publishing Company. *A Biographical History of Darke County, Ohio*. The Lewis Publishing Company, 1900, books.google.com/books/about/A_Biographical_History_of_Darke_County_O.html?id=vg3VAAAAMAAJ

Wilson, Frazer Ells. *History of Darke County, Ohio* 2 Vols. The Hobart Publishing Company, 1914, books.google.com/books/about/History_of_Darke_County_O.html?id=BToVAAAAYAAJ

Delaware County

Beers, F. W. *Atlas of Delaware Co., Ohio*. Beers, Ellis & Soule, 1866, www.historicmapworks.com/Atlas/US/11048/Delaware+County+1866/

Lytle, James R. *20th Century History of Delaware County, Ohio*. Biographical Publishing Company, 1908, archive.org/details/20thcenturyhisto01lytl

Perrin, Henry William. *History of Delaware County and Ohio*. O. L. Baskin & Co., 1880, books.google.com/books/about/History_of_Delaware_County_and_Ohio.html?id=wRAVAAAAYAAJ

Fayette County

Allen, Frank M. *History of Fayette County, Ohio*. B. F. Bowen & Company, Inc., 1914, https://books.google.com/books?id=SBgVAAAAYAAJ&printsec=frontcover&source=gbs_ge_summary_r&cad=0#v=onepage&q&f=false

Everets, L. H. *Illustrated Historical Atlas of Fayette County, Ohio. L. H.* Everets & Co., *1875*, http://www.historicmapworks.com/Atlas.php?cat=Maps&c=US&a=7593

Geauga County

Historical Society of Geauga County. *Pioneer and Genearal History of Geauga County, Ohio*. Historical Society of Geauga County, 1880, https://books.google.com/books?id=Eu0uAAAAYAAJ&printsec=frontcover&source=gbs_ge_summary_r&cad=0#v=onepage&q&f=false

Lake, D. J. *Atlas of Lake and Geauga Counties Ohio*. Titus, Simmons & Titus, 1874, http://www.historicmapworks.com/Atlas/US/7730/Lake+and+Geauga+Counties+1874/

Greene County

Broadstone, Michael A. *History of Greene County, Ohio*. 2 vols. B. F. Bowen & Company, 1918, books.google.com/books/about/History_of_Greene_County_Ohio.html?id=txIVAAAAYAAJ

Dills, R. S. *History of Greene County*. Odell & Mayer, 1881,archive.org/stream/oh-greene-1882-dills#page/n1/mode/2up

Everts, L. H. *Combination Atlas Map of Greene County, Ohio.* L. H. Everts & Co., 1874, www.historicmapworks.com/Atlas/US/9554/Greene+County+1874/

Rogerson, A. E. and Murphy E. J. *Map of Greene County, Ohio.* Anthony D. Byles, 1855, www.loc.gov/resource/g4083g.la000629/

Hamilton County

Emerson, Wm. D. *Map of Hamilton County, Ohio.* C. S. Williams & Son, 1847, https://www.loc.gov/resource/g4083h.la000632/

Harrison, R. H. *Titis' Atlas of Hamilton County, Ohio.* C. O. Titus, 1869, www.historicmapworks.com/Map/US/20654/Title+Page/Cincinnati+and+Hamilton+County+1869/Ohio/

Nelson, S.B. And Runk, J. M. *History of Cininnati And Hamilton County, Ohio.* S. B. Nelson & Co., 1894, books.google.com/books/about/History_of_Cincinnati_and_Hamilton_Count.html?id=alQMAQAAMAAJ

Henry County

Aldrich, Lewis Cass. *History of Henry and Fulton Counties, Ohio.* D. Mason & Co., 1888, books.google.com/books/about/History_of_Henry_and_Fulton_Counties_Ohi.html?id=8SJEAQAAMAAJ

H. H. Hardesty & Co. *Atlas of Henry County, Ohio.* H. H. Hardesty & Co., 1875, www.historicmapworks.com/Atlas/US/10845/Henry+County+1875/

Highland County

Klise, J. W. *The County of Highland.* Northwestern Historical Association, 1902, archive.org/stream/countyhighlanda00houggoog#page/n8/mode/2up

Lake, D. J. *Atlas of Highland County, Ohio.* C. O. Titus, 1871, www.historicmapworks.com/Atlas/US/11119/Highland+County+1871/

Lathrop, J. M. And Penny, H. C. *Atlas of Highland County, Ohio.* H. C. Mead & Co., 1887, www.historicmapworks.com/Atlas/US/9577/Highland+County+1887/

Scott, Daniel. *A History of The Early Settlement of Highland County, Ohio.* The Gazette Office, 1890, books.google.com/books/about/A_History_of_the_Early_Settlement_of_Hig.html?id=C04VAAAAYAAJ

Jackson County

Lake, D. J. *Atlas of Jackson County, Ohio.* Titus, Simmons & Titus, 1875, http://www.historicmapworks.com/Atlas/US/9463/Jackson+County+1875/

Willard, Eugene B. *A Standard History of The Hanging Rock Iron Region of Ohio.* 2 vols. The Lewis Publishing Company, 1916, https://books.google.

com/books?id=gpkqAAAAYAAJ&printsec=frontcover&source=gbs_ge_summary_r&cad=0#v=onepage&q&f=false

Licking County

Beers, F. W. *Atlas of Licking Co., Ohio.* Beers, Soule & Co., 1866, www.historicmapworks.com/Atlas/US/11123/Licking+County+1866/

Hill Jr., N. N. *Hisotry of Licking County, Ohio.* A. A. Graham & Co., 1881, books.google.com/books/about/History_of_Licking_County_O_Its_Past_and.html?id=_Xw8AAAAIAAJ

Montgomery County

Drury, Augustus Waldo. *Hisotry of The City of Dayton And Montgomery County, Ohio.* 2 vols. The S. J. Clarke Publishing Co., 1909, https://books.google.com/books?id=hhObs4HhLlEC&printsec=frontcover&source=gbs_ge_summary_r&cad=0#v=onepage&q&f=false

Lake, D. J. *Titus' Map of Montgomery County Ohio.* C. O. Titus, 1869, https://www.loc.gov/resource/g4083m.la000658/?r=0.652,0.821,0.339,0.213,0

Summit County

Doyle, William B. *Centennial History of Summit County, Ohio.* Biographical Publishing Company, 1908, books.google.com/books/about/Centennial_History_of_Summit_County_Ohio.html?id=tt0yAQAAMAAJ

Perrin, William Henry. *History of Summit County with an Outline Sketch of Ohio.* Baskin & Battey, Historical Publishers, 1881, books.google.com/books/about/History_of_Summit_County.html?id=XpM6AQAAIAAJ

Tackabury, George N. *Combination Atlas Map of Summit County, Ohio.* Tackabury, Mead, & Moffett, 1874, www.historicmapworks.com/Map/US/48004/Title+Page/Summit+County+1874/Ohio/

Tuscarawas County

Everets, L. H. *Combination Atlas Map of Tuscarawas County, Ohio.* L. H. Everets & Co., 1875, http://www.historicmapworks.com/Map/US/50203/Title+Page/Tuscarawas+County+1875/Ohio/

Mansfield, John Brandt. *The History of Tuscarawas County, Ohio.* Warner, Beers & Co., 1884, https://books.google.com/books?id=8d8yAQAAMAAJ&printsec=frontcover&source=gbs_ge_summary_r&cad=0#v=onepage&q&f=false

Vinton County

Lake, D. J. *Atlas of Vinton Co., Ohio.* Titus, Simmons, & Titus, 1876, www.historicmapworks.com/Atlas/US/9375/Vinton+County+1876/

Willard, Eugene B., et al. *A Standard History of The Hanging Rock Iron Region of Ohio.* 2 vols. The Lewis Publishing Company, 1916,

books.google.com/books/about/A_Standard_History_of_the_Hanging_Rock_I.html?id=gpkqAAAAYAAJ

Warren County

Bone, Frank A. *Complete Atlas of Warren County, Ohio.* Frank A. Bone, 1891, www.historicmapworks.com/Map/US/174701/Title+Page/Warren+County+1891/Ohio/

Everts, L. H. *Combination Atlas Map of Warren County, Ohio.* L. H. Everts, 1875, www.historicmapworks.com/Map/US/1256383/Title+Page/Warren+County+1875/Ohio/

Beers, W. H. *The History of Warren County, Ohio.* W. H. Beers & Co., 1882, books.google.com/books/about/The_History_of_Warren_County_Ohio.html?id=nbLLGwAACAAJ

Websites with General Resources

Bridges—bridgehunter.com

Cemeteries—findagrave.com

Genealogy—familysearch.org

Ghost Legends—hauntedplaces.org

Iron Furnaces—oldindustry.org

Maps—loc.gov/maps/?q=ohio

Mills—oldmills.scificincinnati.com/

Post Offices—postalhistory.com

Railroads—abandonedrails.com

Schools—oldohioschools.com

Train Stations—west2k.com